Land of Ch

Stories of Struggle & Solidarity from Wales

Edited by
Dr. Gemma June Howell

Afterword by
Prof. K.E. Howell

with cover images by
Rachel Oliver

Oppression with its multitude of lords
Is waving its banners;
Now or never, brave men of Wales,
Let us go to the battle, to the battle;

—Daniel James

Culture Matters Co-Operative Ltd. promotes a socialist and progressive approach to art, culture and politics. See www.culturematters.org.uk

Text and images copyright © the contributors
Cover art © Rachel Oliver
Typesetting by Alan Morrison
ISBN 978-1-912710-46-1

Acknowledgements

Culture Matters would like to give a special thanks to the Calon Lan Centre in Morriston, the Cultural Institute, Miners' Library and Richard Burton Archives at Swansea University, the Cardiff Stop the War Coalition and the Wales Democratic Kurdish People's Assembly. We'd also like to acknowledge other publishers for permission to reprint some of the contributions, including Carreg Gwalch, Parthian, *Planet* and *The Welsh Agenda*.

Contents

Introduction

By Gemma June Howell

As a record of resistance, this colourful collection of bold artworks and documentary photography as well as insightful, enlightening, and poignant creative pieces, speeches, journalism, and memoir, is a celebration of the diverse collectanea of underrepresented and working-class voices from Wales.

The working classes are often stereotyped as one body—one class—with representations of social class seen in terms of binary oppositions; where one class is like this, the other is not. But working-class culture shouldn't be seen as one single entity; surely it should be understood as an accumulation of life experiences amassed over time and place. It is not one body. It is not a 'structure' nor a 'category'[1], it is a plethora of historical phenomena born of shared experiences, and, as such, those experiences should be interpreted from the perspective of those who live them.

As identity has become synonymous with political action, with movements seeking common ground within the intersections of oppression, this anthology makes a stand against the insidious tactics of cultural imperialism and its erasure and misappropriation of underrepresented and working-class identities, and ultimately serves to preserve a collective of marginalised 'others' through the lens of their lived experiences.

The work of Daniel James is largely unknown. He, like many of the contributors in this anthology, is an unsung hero of the arts in Wales. He started work at the age of 13 as a labourer, then a steelworker, and alongside this backbreaking, unforgiving toil, he began to write political poetry in Welsh[2]. In his poem, 'Freedom's War Cry,' James appeals to his reader to fight against 'oppression and its multitude of lords', and referring to the 'bravery of our forefathers' [and mothers], he urges us to 'claim our rights'. ***Land of Change: Stories of Struggle & Solidarity from Wales*** does exactly that: it draws on Wales' cultural origins of struggle and solidarity; unearths a wealth of unheard voices waiting in the margins; and challenges dominant ideologies by shining a light

---

[1] E. P. Thompson, *The Making of the English Working Class*, (1963, p. 11).

[2] Daniel James was taught by D.W. Thomas, an elder at Mynyddbach Chapel and began to write verse under the pseudonym Dafydd Mynyddbach, but he later assumed the Bardic name Gwyrosydd (Source: Calon Lan Centre).

on the historical reality of working-class life worlds in Wales and beyond. Sadly, in a contemporary, post-industrial environment, the visibility of working-class lives are portrayed as dysfunctional, dependent on the state and generally a social problem that needs to be solved by the professional middle classes or the philanthropic cultured upper classes. Traditionally culture has been viewed as luxury, defined as something exclusively for middle or upper-class tastes, and in his essay, *Culture is Ordinary*[3], socialist critic Raymond Williams questions its exclusionary nature, as elitist ideology deems what is worthy of cultural or educational consideration. In Tony Webb's account of Marxist revolutionary, 'Dad Ern', he shares an intimate portrayal of the self-educated unsung hero, and legendary figure from the village of Pentre-Dwr, where: 'most houses took the *Daily Worker* newspaper'. A historically relevant, inherited experience, Webb's account is a valued contribution to working-class culture in Wales, focusing on the relationships between *real* people living in times of real struggle.

In Mark S. Redfern's unflinching analysis of the documentary *Swansea Love Story* he slams the film as 'an overlooked landmark for the portrayal of Welsh culture in the media for the wrong reasons. It is an indispensable case study in cack-handed poverty porn, laying bare how we are viewed by the London-centric media class'. Managing the isolated 'debauchery of a new generation' of the less fortunate, without consideration for deeper socio-political issues at play, the film ignores that such issues are endemic in post-industrial communities across Britain. Redfern highlights how the film 'relies on crude stereotypes' and sensationalism, which only serves to undermine individual subjectivity, and deny the Welsh working classes the ability to collectively transcend and *become* the Wales it chooses to be. Rebecca Lowe's 'Being Poor is Not a Life Choice' comments on the social impact and blinkered mainstream view of the working poor as her parents' 'upwardly mobile friend' points to poverty as a life choice: an opinion reminiscent of Victorian Britain, where the exploitation of the working classes has returned us to levels of poverty witnessed during this Malthusian economic period. As Lowe points out, 'Food poverty, cramped and overcrowded living conditions, money worries and job insecurity, plus the stress of working multiple jobs on minimal incomes—all of these add up to a less healthy lifestyle. Being poor is deadly'. With working-class people labouring under zero-hours contracts in an unpredictable gig economy, 'the

[3] Raymond Williams, *Culture is Ordinary* (1958).

rich have money sitting in investments making them more money'. There are record numbers of working families living in abject poverty, relying on food banks to survive, and Rachel Oliver's depiction of Theresa May in her outstanding digital artwork *If Only I had a Heart*, accurately illustrates Lowe's exposé. And, in other stories, such as John Frost's account of 'Working in a Factory during Covid,' we see the degradation of home and migrant workers, in a blatant dismissal for the value of human life and safety in favour of production and profit. In Gerhard Kress' 'Immigrants Built Merthyr', and the accompanying photography, we get a sense of pride, and solidarity with our fellow global citizens, as 'we are all immigrants, just as we all 'belong.''

The forty-four stories told in this anthology stretch back to include over thirty years of political activity and personal struggle. With contributions from Tim Evans, Tim Richards, Des Mannay, Jacqueline Jones, Taz Rahman and Eric Ngalle Charles documenting and commenting on the impact of seismic social changes with 'ordinary people winning victories against the odds' (Rhoda Thomas). From the breakdown of trade unions and post-industrialisation to the reduction of the Welfare State under Conservative-led austerity. The wars on "terror" and rise of Trump and Bo-Jo's contagious neo-fascism, and its consequential spread of xenophobia. Police brutality, violence against women seen in Samantha Mansi's life-writing, illustrating her experiences of living in refuge. As well as the systematic abuse of women, with a string of murders and sexual abuse scandals exposing a pervasive culture of misogyny. Zoe John explores the degradation and humiliation of women and 'other' in Mixed Martial Arts, and issues surrounding toxic masculinity are highlighted in Jon Doyle's 'Be the Best.' A stark, and contemporary memoir by Summar Jade exposes the double standards embodied within sexist narratives. And, more recently, the impending perils of climate change, disease, and war; with disaster capitalists profiting from Brexit and the global pandemic. Rachel Oliver, Tracey Rhys, Osian Grifford, David Collyer, Alan Perry and Richard Blacklaw Jones' artwork and photography provide a vital illustrative commentary, while Xavier Panadès i Blas and Gareth Twamley's fictional pieces envisage a bleak, dystopian view of the future.

But, while all of these recent events have fanned the flames of widespread distrust, conspiracy theories and political polarisation, there couldn't be a more pressing time for resistance and solidarity ... so much so, that the government are now restricting our right to protest! Evans' 'Battle of Trafalgar Square' gives a vivid account of the 1990 Poll Tax uprising.

> By 1989-90 the British working class had been given a sustained kicking for a long time. Anger levels were very high. The poll tax uprising was like a lightning conductor for years of pent-up frustration and fury that on 31 March exploded onto the streets.

As he triumphantly declares, 'The poll tax riot marked not just the end of the poll tax, but the end of Thatcher'. Since the 1980s, neoliberal capitalism, imperialism and tyrannical leaders have certainly left an ideological mark: a legacy where entrenched individualistic and self-serving values are accepted as common-sense—part of the social fabric! But it's the working classes, the underrepresented, silenced and marginalised who have disproportionately felt the brunt of such seismic changes: it is the working classes that have risen to the challenge. Yet, despite the present immediacy, and overarching need to fight for social equality and human rights, the public perception of protesters remains largely negative. Raymond Williams[4] attributes such negative traits to the evolution of the masses: initially consisting of the *mob*, the masses, or working classes, have therefore inherited damaging features associated with mob mentality. 'The masses', he says, 'are other people'[5]; and he examines how our interpretation of 'the man on the street' is a 'collective image', however 'we know, all the time, our differences to him'[6]. Such differences are only exacerbated by an individualized notion of identity, however as Williams states, 'there are in fact no masses; there are only ways of seeing people as masses'.[7]

Working-class people have their own cultures. They have their own organic intellectuals, writers and artists who can, and *are* finding common ground to unite and release themselves from an engrained 'false consciousness'[8] maintained by a hegemonic ideology embedded in imperialism, colonialism, and elitism. Within these pages, you will find contributions from Wales' very own organic writers, intellectuals, and artists, which include excellent paint on canvas pieces from Gustavius Payne, Sarah Oneill, M.J. and Fionn Wilson; revealing memoir from Alys Einion and Margot Morgan; Jon Gower's tender portrayal of poverty in South America, whereas Mike Jenkins, J. Brookes, Karl

---

[4] Raymond Williams, *Culture & Society* (1963/2017).
[5] (ibid) (1963/2017 p. 393).
[6] (ibid).
[7] (ibid)
[8] Antonio Gramsci, *Selections from the Prison Notebooks of Antonio Gramsci* (1971).

Francis, Rob Mimpriss, Philip John, Phil Knight, lloyd robson, Leon Noakes all shed light on the past, present and future of Welsh culture. Phillipa Brown's outstanding artwork formed the publicity for the CSOS, and Gwenno Dafydd (who was the host for the 2017 Sister March in Cardiff) has songs in Welsh, English, and Scottish Gaelic that burst from the pages; whereas Maj Ikle provides a tender account of rural life in Wales, and Rhys Trimble give a bilingual account of his neurodivergent experiences of Covid-19.

Queer and nonbinary poet, Sierra Moulinié, gives a provocative speech, 'Child', where they express their indignation of being the product 'of a system of government so corrupt that families starve, or beg, or steal, because a parent's benefits have been sanctioned after they were too sick for a pointless meeting, whilst billionaires and CEOs are allowed to keep doing anything they want, simply because they went to schools with fancy ties and silly handshakes.' A stand-out piece in the anthology, which matches the vehemence of Krystal Lowe, who conveys the finer, often over-looked, details of her lived experiences, when she demands 'room' in the sector she loves: 'My place is in every space where art is made and performed; my creativity and my work will only improve the world at large .... If your shows cannot showcase me—Write. New. Shows. Tell the truth. You prefer racism to change—don't you?' Kate Cleaver's 'Am I Black Enough?' highlights the hypocrisy, damaging lack of education, and ignorance seen in the white supremacist comments on her Facebook feed; and how she bravely endures this to remain grounded and informed for her personal fight against racism. The personal trials here clearly demonstrate a greater need to struggle together and show solidarity in the face of hatred and misinformation.

In Rhoda Thomas' 'Working-class Woman' she talks of how political struggles are often depicted in the media as isolated or localised: 'keeping battles atomised is one way of preventing people from seeing what is really happening'. But, the murder of George Floyd, and subsequent resurgence of BLM activism has intensified criticism of widespread institutional racism, including within the publishing sector, which has 'resulted in the industry being shaken to its core ... taking systematic racism seriously for the first time'[9]. Yet, despite this 'real awakening'[10], which could be compared to that of the 1800s humanitarian reformers, we are reaching a transformative climax, and it could be said that in

---

[9] Bernadine Evaristo, *Manifesto on Never Giving Up* (2021 p. 176).
[10] E.P. Thompson, *The Making of the English Working Class* (1963 p. 376).

today's post-truth, digi-woke environment, the doors of domination are being edged open; allowing the marginalised other to be heard by a global audience. And despite the incessant avalanche of negative news, backlit with political corruption and hypocrisy, spawning a generation of cynics and conspirators, there is *still* hope in the form of solidarity. Anti-austerity, anti-racist and feminist movements, such as the Cardiff People's Assembly, the Cardiff Sisters of Solidarity, who joined the Global Women's strike, 'calling for solidarity between women—women of colour, indigenous, working class, disabled, migrant, Muslim, lesbian, queer and trans women' (Claudia Boes), and the Black Lives Matter Movement heralding a new generation of activists and political orators, who are joining together to elevate the voices of the powerless. Zero Racism Champion, Queen Niche, who in her opening speech for the BLM demonstrations in Cardiff last year, speaks with conviction, clarity, and passion: 'We need unity to end the division/ Updated policies, they need revision/ We need to understand this land is not just for the white man!' In Adam Johannes' account of Day 90 of Kurdish activist, Imam Sis' hunger strike, he signs off with: 'If the nationalist, racist, sexist states of this capitalist and imperialist system provide each other with all sorts of support, we, as the peoples of the world, must be able to put our differences and ideological discussions aside to struggle alongside each other and to stand beside one another in solidarity and support.' And, as Tim Evans augments: 'International solidarity is more powerful than we think'.

Works by Bronwen Davies, Caroline Richards and H Raven Rose take an eco-feminist approach, drawing on Welsh mythology and nature writing to document humanity's demise and potential to heal, prevail. In an amorous idealisation of Wales' Neolithic past, Bronwen contrasts her natural surroundings with a digitally reliant future. In her accompanying photograph, her son does 'cartwheels on the edge of the earth', representing the fragility of our future in this increasingly turbulent and unpredictable world. But there is still a sense of strength, hope and collective resilience, as 'hazel branches entwine, supporting each other', and a 'family of elm fuse together', despite having 'found herself among totems and relics from a distant past, with a promise on her lips to never let the same mistakes happen again'. Elements of collective trauma, and individual struggle are felt in H Raven Rose's piece, where 'the woman might forge a path to herself/ through the dark forest of her pain/ Home to Wales, where one might heal the heart,/ Hold the grief-stricken Inner Child(ren)'. Arron Kuiper mobilizes paint in his unique, world-first sculptural paintings, which stand proudly alongside the stories within these pages. His scenic piece, 'Of Water Course' is a 'surreal depiction of a Welsh water course from mountain tributary to valley river, communicating how numerous ecosystems depend upon them'. Such ecosystems could be applied to a variety of settings, including Welsh culture, and 'our human position in terms of understanding, overview, and responsibility'.

The anthology aptly concludes with Caroline Richards' 'Rough Guide to Being Human,' where she declares that a 'healthy world needs wonderful humans. Stick up for yourself and for others too, find your power and use it for good'. *Land of Change* is certainly a source of power for many. It is a homage to the 'wonderful humans' of Wales, and as an essential record of voices, past and present, this anthology is a worthwhile contribution to the heart, soul, and substance of Wales.

Tim Evans, *Portrait of Daniel James*

"Hear the trumpet call to war,
Tearing the bosom of the breeze;
The Goddess of Freedom loudly calling
Her children to the battle.
Oppression with its multitude of lords
Is waving its banners;
Now or never, brave men of Wales,
Let us go to the battle, to the battle;
May the bravery of our forefathers
Kindle our bosom
Like a fire, to drive us on,
Until we claim our rights;
If we are defeated by oppression
Let no one tell the tale;
We will die bravely in the war
On the bosom of Freedom."

'Freedom's War Cry' by Daniel James
Translation by Luke Dawson (Calon Centre)

Working-class Woman

By Rhoda Thomas

Everyone thinks I'm posh. They always have. When I was at primary school, my classmates used to call me 'skinny' and 'smelly' and refused to let me join their games. I always spoke well and I think this was because my grandmother had been in service, so we knew all about which knives and forks went where, and how to have perfect manners and always be well turned out. Other women would run down to the shops in slippers and hair curlers, but my mother would never dream of doing that.

We lived in a corner house behind a factory in Hither Green in south-east London. My mother kept the front room for visitors and we lived in the 'morning-room', along with a cat and a Raeburn stove. There was a bath-house shed attached to it with a corrugated iron roof and in the winter, it was freezing. My father mended people's televisions, it was the Windrush era and many of his customers were black. In south London in the 1960s, it was a time of increasing racial tension. He made good money and employed an engineer and two delivery drivers. We hardly ever had a holiday, because my father couldn't leave his business. Some years, we went to my grandmother's bungalow near Ramsgate—it was full of spiders and dust from being shut up all year and my mother hated it.

In the mornings, I got up first and went down to the kitchen, I'd climb on a chair with a long spill and light the Ascot heater so that I could have hot water to wash in. Then I'd cook some porridge before walking to school, something I was scared of because I thought we were rich and that I could be kidnapped for a ransom. The message to keep away from strangers rang in my ears.

I left home at 19 and got a job as a nursing assistant in a psychiatric hospital. My mother said she thought I needed my 'head tested' to work with 'those people'—scarcely encouraging and again, hostile to anything she didn't understand. I think she also resented that I'd abandoned my role looking after my younger siblings, but she never said.

In those days you could get an independent grant if you worked for 3 years, so that's how I was able to go to Goldsmiths College in 1976—to study psychology. That year was also the beginning of Richard Hoggart's tenure there—he was all for working-class culture and making higher education more accessible. Whilst there, I not only got my degree, but also had music lessons and got another grade on the piano, because they had teachers on site and practice rooms.

My parents thought that everyone should have to struggle for every penny the way they had, and once when I approached them for support during final exams, they made it clear that I had breached a sacrosanct family rule by daring to ask for help.

In 1981, I arrived in Cardiff and rented a flat in a big Victorian house. Two black girls lived upstairs, and I soon learned that they were 'on the game', what we might now call sex work. I don't know how much agency they felt about their line of work. There were lots of fights and arguments from upstairs. At the back of the house, there was a family who got regular visits from the police. I had a teaching job at the local college and walked up and down the hill every day carrying books and a packed lunch. Students would often sail past me in their cars. I was very lonely. The girls upstairs had white fur carpets, a leather settee, and a glass coffee table, they found it strange that even on my teaching salary I just had bare floorboards and all my books remained in crates from the greengrocer's. I had an old piano and the people in the house I lived in sometimes knocked on the door to come in and listen to me playing.

It was after many years and three marriages later, that I met my current partner in Swansea. None of my husbands had ever had any money and I lost my home twice. My second husband (who died from cancer) came from a family of 10 based in Battersea. He had left school at 14. From time to time, he did a bit of night-shift care work. He was a renowned painter and painted the most exquisite land and seascapes and flower pictures. Money came in from sales of these, sporadically. My third husband had gone to the Royal College of Art but developed a lot of illnesses, culminating in a leg amputation shortly before he died. My brother, a talented saxophonist, lived on the breadline and died at 51 from cancer. Neither education nor creativity protects you from ill-health or economic hardship.

I rarely had more than that month's wages and I had to borrow from the bank to keep my life going. I never had any money for fun—and once my daughter was born, I didn't go out socially for 16 years.

I was on short-term contracts for more than 25 years (over half my working life), so promotion perpetually eluded me. In any case, I did not fit the criteria. For a working-class woman in my position, it was impossible to build the track record of publishing, international conferences and grant applications required on top of day-to-day teaching and responsibilities. At one time, I was teaching 1,000 students a week, and for 11 years, I travelled the length and breadth of Wales as part of my job. To occupy the hours spent on the road, I was learning to sing and learning Welsh and I would drive across Snowdonia, the Beacons and the Black Mountains practising both at the top of my voice.

As a woman, I experienced both poverty and prejudice. I was running women's studies courses, sitting on equal opportunities committees, studying gender and sexuality. But I was also driving home through the dark, worrying about financial survival, too late to see my child, too tired to sort things out with partners, too unavailable to talk to neighbours, sometimes suicidal. All the work I was doing was against the tide and I was always exhausted. I had made my way into an academic world without money, without contacts, without knowledge of how it worked. I was always in struggle, my head down, getting the work done—indeed, my life depended on it. I couldn't see that my own strength was something to value. I thought that my misfortune was my fault.

I worked to make other people's projects succeed, not my own, but I hadn't recognised that using people's energy to make profits for the rich was a universal practice. Yes, through the trade union, I had fought for better pay and against department closures, but I hadn't fully understood this was part of a much bigger picture. Keeping battles atomised is one way of preventing people from seeing what is really happening.

Around the age of 50, I rented an unfurnished house near Brynmill Park, close to my work. I had bought a cooker, installed a washing-machine, laid new floor tiles instead of a smoky old carpet, only to find that the landlord had changed his mind and wanted us out at the end of 6 months. I was experiencing the unfairness of the system that favours those with property and treats those without it as dispensable.

Chronic stress from money worries and insecurity damages health. Eventually I developed diabetes 2, avoidable if my life had been easier and if I hadn't reached for food and drink as a way of coping. Like millions of women, my life has involved a significant burden of unpaid emotional and domestic labour, little of which has been catalogued or recognised. The pension age was raised for women who were born in the 1950s so that I've had to go into my later years with debt once again on my back, too late in life to earn again.

For many, it has been much worse than this. Before lockdown, in the Uplands and Swansea city centre, the number of people begging for money or sleeping rough was increasing. This was the result of intentional political neglect across the UK. Giving a few pence here and there was not enough. This was a system that wasted human potential and left people with little support in a brutally competitive environment. It seemed to me that the best thing I could do was to work with others for change. This life we live is not 'normal' and for many is intolerable. This could be a wonderful world—why isn't it?

My parents thought that all of us were fundamentally alone. I knew that this was not true and that I had to fight against that message. In recent times, I have been inspired by seeing hundreds of thousands of people joining the movement for change. I now know this is not just my struggle.

By digging into real history rather than what I'd been taught at school, I discovered that people have risen up again and again, taking things into their own hands, building solidarity, often winning victories against the odds. Joining together with others is the most powerful instrument for change we have as well as being the most joyful way to live.

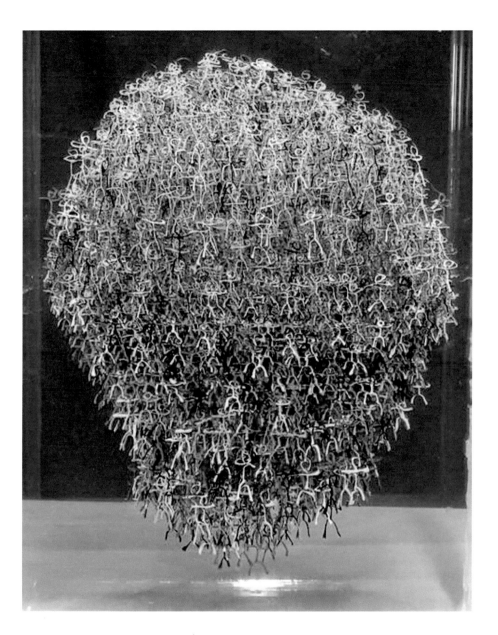

Arron Kuiper, *Cloud*

When Vice Came to Swansea

By Mark S. Redfern

Fionn Wilson, *Port Talbot Steel Works*

If you've watched a couple of videos on YouTube from the hip, cool, edgy media outlet Vice, chances are you'll get some recommendations for their most popular videos in your sidebar. *The Cannibal Warlords of Liberia. Suicide Forest in Japan. The Biggest Ass in Brazil.* Their reach is global, and they love taboos. One of the most eye-catching videos has the ominous title *Teenage Heroin Epidemic.* The thumbnail lures watchers in with a picture of a gaunt man strung-out, dosed off his skull on smack. Drooped eyelids. Mouth agape. He couldn't tell the difference between Vice's camera lens and a rubber duck.

The hour-long documentary is a story about young people living precariously around Swansea, balancing their addictions and personal lives without money or shelter. It's called *Swansea Love Story*, made for Vice in 2010 and repackaged for YouTube under a more provocative title. The film has had millions of views and is one of the most popular documentaries of Vice's entire library. The YouTube version continues to attract many comments from across the globe, including thousands from 2019 alone—some express sympathy for the participants in the documentary, but many ridicule them, their accents, Swansea, and Wales. Other viewers attempt to trawl for the documentary protagonists on Facebook, to see how they are doing now. The documentary is an overlooked landmark for the portrayal of Welsh culture in the media for all the wrong reasons. It is indispensable as a case study in cack-handed poverty porn, laying bare how we are viewed by the London-centric media class. The directors, Andy Capper and Leo Leigh, donned their pith helmets and went hunting for a story in the badlands of Swansea.

The thumbnail is taken from a sequence in the first five minutes where the subjects shoot up behind a rubbish bin. It's graphic. Long-time user Andrew nods from the dope in a side-alley after he injects. When he regains some brain function, he stumbles onto his mountain bike and zig-zags off into the distance. This gross-out sequence is the hook of the documentary. The rest of the film revolves around the abusive relationship of Cornelius and Amy, the titular *Love Story*. The filler scenes woven throughout, however, betray how the producers really view Welsh people and their culture.

To begin with, the fringe characters are treated as the oafish comic relief throughout the documentary. When we first meet recently clean Lee, he struggles to figure out how to attach his lapel mic. The producers splice in a blooper where he tries to put this alien device to his ear like an earpiece. During the introduction to another offbeat character, Clint, he farts. The producers paste this in for comedic effect whilst he's talking about the addiction destroying his life. 'I just want the chance to be a daddy, yeah? It wouldn't be fair on my children if I was to go: "Oh, that's my daddy that is." "Ah, but your daddy's a junkie!"', he says later. Months after the film was made, Vice journalist Alison Severs contacted Clint to write a follow-up. He was clean but told Severs that his kids had been ridiculed in school as a result of his portrayal: 'Last year, when we made the film, my kids' friends were calling me a "druggie" and giving them hassle in the playground.'[1] Indulgent close-ups of him injecting heroin probably didn't help his family problems either.

Some might suggest the gags were just ham-fisted levity, though the producers don't sound too empathetic. Capper wrote about the closing scenes, in which a withdrawing user called Kristian tags along: 'While we were

---

[1] https://www.vice.com/en_uk/article/qbwwdv/clint-ryan-jones-interviewswansea-love-story

shooting them on the beach Kristian kept puking up and then going: "It's all right boys," in this weird camp voice. The shots were (black) comedy gold but didn't make the cut in the end.'[2] Jokes can make a difficult subject easier to digest, but this is just mockery.

Aside from the main characters, the producers also visit places around town that are supposed to be typical of modern Wales. In a segment outside Swansea train station, we see a hostile crowd ready to ruck, and a few, unclear shots of an anti-racist counter-demonstration. The event is later described by Capper in an article published on CNN's website as the camera crew having 'stumbled into a race riot',[3] making it sound as if this was a common occurrence around town. By all accounts, in reality the one-off protest was small and organised by an impotent gaggle of Welsh Defence League hooligans, an offshoot of the much more popular English Defence League. The BBC estimated that the counter-demonstration attracted around 200 protesters against the demonstration, dwarfing the estimated 60 WDL protesters.[4] The documentary gives little indication of this context.

Prior to this, the cameras had visited a traditional working men's club. Decent ways to earn money, like manufacturing and labouring, have been replaced by hard drugs and debasement, the men tell us. There is then a smash cut to the local strip-bar where young women wrapped in fishnets perform for punters under strobe lights. Everything that the old guard of the working class despises goes on there, with the club even operating out of a renovated factory as a final insult. Interviews with the dancers show they are more than happy with their career choices, and that their mothers and grandmothers envy their confidence. Nevertheless, promiscuity and sexual vulgarity have often been the backbone of the 'chav' stereotype. We're shown the dissonance between the old, refined, dignified working class of the city and the debauchery of the new generation. Although the condescension of the old working men appears to be the punchline, the overall thrust of the documentary is that drug-taking and sexual degradation is the instinctual Welsh reaction to poverty. The pretence on the part of the producers that their film offers a comprehensive picture

---

[2] https://www.vice.com/en_uk/article/5g5d98/a-swansea-scrapbook
[3] http://edition.cnn.com/2010/WORLD/europe/02/21/vbs.swansea.love.story/index.html
[4] http://news.bbc.co.uk/1/hi/wales/south_west/8311673.stm

of working-class south-Walian society as a whole (rather than a problematic portrayal of the lives of a small minority) is accentuated by the incongruous footage and audio of Dunvant Male Voice Choir singing *Si Hei Lwli Mabi* alongside some of the most desperate scenes of drug use.

The most uneasy sequences are shown as the film draws to a close. In one uncomfortable scene, Amy, drunk and off-guard, reveals harrowing details of how she was sexually abused as a child, and her mother's complicity in it. Some may see the capturing on film of such a heart-breakingly painful disclosure as the sign of a great journalist, yet the underlying problems in Welsh society that explain why Amy has been forced into such an unhealthy lifestyle because of her childhood are left unexplored. Maybe this was too much of a downer to mention. When slotted into a documentary whose other set-pieces are fascist marches and vodka-drenched strippers, the details of abuse are just another attraction in this horror-show.

Not long after the film had been released South Wales Police swept in and collared twenty-six drug users from around Swansea town centre, among them Cornelius. 'It took our film for the authorities to do something about the heroin use in Swansea,' said one of the directors, 'and this isn't the best way'.[5] So what went wrong? Hearing Capper and Leigh speak in promotional interviews makes them sound like Jane Goddall coaxing the apes down from the canopy. Capper said to *Wales Online*: 'I suppose outside of drug workers, other addicts or the police there's no-one around to show them a friendly face or even look them in the eye. So, they welcomed us—we were a novelty to them, I guess.'[6] When looking into the backgrounds of the directors we start to understand that their lives are also a novelty to the vast majority of Welsh people.

Capper was the co-director of the Vice brand in the UK. He spent his formative years at Scarisbrick Hall School, Lancashire. The edgy journalist listed his activities in the school in his profile on LinkedIn: 'Being yelled at. Glue sniffing.' His parents wouldn't have wanted him to squander his time there; an education at Scarisbrick Hall would nowadays set you back a cool

---

[5] https://www.vice.com/en_uk/article/xd4q73/swansea-love-story-vs-the-law
[6] https://www.walesonline.co.uk/news/wales-news/shock-documentary-uncovers-scale-heroin-2064921

£11,000 a year. Capper's privilege pales in comparison to the cushty childhood of his codirector. Leo Leigh is the son of wealthy award-winning film director Mike Leigh, and he was sent to a swanky private school too. Leigh boarded at Northease Manor School in East Sussex, with fees now almost triple that of his colleague.[7] When Leigh the Younger spoke to *The Guardian* about his blossoming film career, just starting out with *Swansea Love Story* at the time, he came across as totally unaware of his luck: 'You know what, films are either good or they're not. I don't think people are going to say, "Well his films are shit but his dad is Mike Leigh," and give me loads of money.'[8]

Ignorance of working-class life has led them to rely on crude stereotypes. Documentaries like *Benefits Street* or *Skint* play to classist tropes and *Swansea Love Story* follows many of the same beats. Despite sequences that attempt to convey tenderness and sympathy, Vice ultimately portrays Cornelius and Amy as obnoxious criminals, Lee as a moron, and Clint as a buffoon; without full exploration of the struggles these people faced from early childhood. Labelling a film a documentary tells viewers that these depictions are truthful. And as to the society that produced these characters, the best explanation that Capper and Leigh could scrape together were vague references to Thatcher and capitalism washed down with an obligatory visit to a disused colliery. Our presence on the UK stage is so insignificant the entire essence of Welsh society can be summed up in a few trite platitudes.

The BBC later made a much grimier film that managed to be more sympathetic. Producers followed three men in the depths of their addictions, once again, around Swansea. Anxiety, abscesses, and amputations may have all been on show for the camera, yet the core message of the documentary, part of the 2016 *Drugs Map of Britain* series, was that alienation was one of the main drivers behind long-term drug abuse. Somehow, Leigh thinks that his approach to *Swansea Love Story* made it a real thought-provoker too. Speaking to the *Evening Standard*, he gave himself props for doing immersion journalism so well: 'You live with the subject and get a more balanced picture, putting in the human emotions and personalities that tend to get washed away in the news reports.'[9] The resulting film shows no signs of this.

---

[7] http://leoleigh.com/blog/page/4/

[8] https://www.theguardian.com/film/2009/dec/17/leo-leigh-swansea-love-story1.

[9] https://www.standard.co.uk/showbiz/starinterviews/my-dad-mike-leigh-said-ifyou-

But what can we expect? Vice's style, after all, is sensationalism. Blood-and-guts guerrilla filmmaking is their hallmark, and in her book *Merchants of Truth*, Jill Abramson gives the true essence of Vice's brand as 'half-baked reportage on depraved situations'.[10] Advertisers seeking to reach the youth crowd are attracted to Vice; their edgy reporting has won them the lion's share of the market. YouTube has found their content so useful in drawing viewers to their platform that they were paying Vice 'tens of millions'[11] of dollars to host their documentaries on the platform. Being outlandish pays the bills and the exotic degradation of Swansea's heroin subculture was perfect for the commissioners back in London. Humiliating depictions of people at their lowest ebb therefore can be replayed into perpetuity, often long after they have turned their lives around.

The lives of those on Swansea's streets are light-years away from the gilded habitat Leigh and Capper came from. This is one explanation for why the protagonists of the film are portrayed as creatures of council estate swamplands. Another is the bombast of Vice's signature style. Add to this the dire representation of Welsh culture on the UK and world stage and it's a calamity (MTV's *The Valleys* and *Dirty Sanchez* are not-so-proud national moments). In Wales, the news media landscape is scant, to say the least. What little reportage on drug users there existed was surely dwarfed by this cartoonish, low-effort project. There is no recourse to counter the myths Vice has broadcast across the globe either. Even Vice's Japanese site has published the film. The false image of Swansea, and by implication Wales as a whole, is that of a poor nation that in times of recession has taken to drugs and depravity like a starving lion to a gazelle.

Wales doesn't need dirty-realist B-movies to tackle drug-related deaths. It needs drug law reform and decriminalisation: drug consumption rooms, improved access to heroin-assisted treatment (the prescription of substitutes such as methadone) and to rehabilitation and counselling services. It needs a news media that can highlight issues of drug harm to stimulate debate on solutions. Until then, we are at the mercy of companies like Vice

---

become-an-actor-ill-break-your-legs-6751784.html.
[10] Jill Abramson, *Merchants of Truth: Inside the News Revolution* (Bodley Head, 2019), p.47
[11] As above, p.158

making films so lucrative, yet so repugnant and morally desolate, there's not a lot else to compare them to but hipster variants of the *Bumfights* producers and iconic bear-baiter Jeremy Kyle. The need for law reform and a responsible media approach is now ever more urgent. According to Public Health Wales, drug fatalities are at record levels, with deaths from drug poisoning increasing by almost 80% in the last decade—and Swansea has the highest rate of deaths in Wales.[12]

Capper mentioned in an interview to IndieWire in 2012 that there was a *Swansea Love Story, Part 2* in the works.[13] If you see him and his hunting party prowling the streets, camera locked and loaded, you must run for your dignity.

First published in *Planet* 236.

---

[12] https://www.theguardian.com/society/2019/sep/22/too-late-save-her-swansea-drug-death-epidemic-wales.

[13] https://www.indiewire.com/2012/09/tiff-futures-vice-editor-andy-capper-goes-behind-the-camera-to-shed-a-light-on-snoop-dogg-in-reincarnated-241778/

Alan Perry, *Running Man*

The High Life

By Bronwen Davies

Bronwen Davies, *Cartwheels on the Edge of the Earth*

Healing and health are priorities alongside celebrating and nurturing the natural landscape. Old coal mining sites are now green spaces. Children paddle in streams under the dappled shade of oak trees, stepping barefoot around rusted iron wheels, bits of old railway track, pieces of coal and broken red bricks. The Gethin Forest above Cwmbach sprawls across two counties and links with parts of Mountain Ash, Merthyr, and Aberdare. An abandoned tunnel runs through the mountain to Pentrebach, the mouth of which has a permanent cold damp breeze blowing through. Mossy mounds abound shrouding piles of ancient stones. Pine needle paths sprinkled with lichen invitingly lead to clay pools. Shangri Las emerge, laced with seasonal treasures like Himalayan balsam, purple heather, holly heavy with red berries, wimberries for summer pies, nuts and blackberries in the Autumn. The sonic and outdoor landscapes surrounding Bronwen do not change quickly beyond the rhythm of the moons and seasons. She has found herself among totems and relics from a distant past, with a promise on her lips to never let the same mistakes happen again.

There is a high edge of the Cwmbach mountain over-looking the Cynon valley. On a clear night occasionally, someone lights a small fire up there that can be seen dancing on the skyline, like a hill-fort beacon. A view perhaps the neolithic ancestors would have gazed upon during their era living on the high grounds surrounding Cwmbach. It is on this edge of the hill (affectionately nicknamed 'Deadbush Mountain') where (a phone free) Bronwen reaches for her son's iPad (with the battery on 1%) and takes a photo of him practising cartwheels on the edge of the world. Below, everything else, tiny and far away.

Up on the high grounds where the ancestors roam is where Bronwen feels free, where everything makes sense.

Decaying trees blister with health boosting polypore, turkey tail to strengthen immunity sprouts from rotting logs. Hazel branches entwine supporting each other, a family of Elm are fused together. Streams tinkle beneath giant ferns, diamonds drip over glossy stones in frosty glades with cyclamen carpets. A buzzard swoops from its hunting perch and glides beneath the canopy, through the trees at eye level flying straight as an arrow, out of the woods. Sunbeams stream through tiny holes in a tall branchless hollow beech tree, the golden lasers pierce through musky bark dust. A stout raven croaks and circles the clear blue sky.

This is the high life, this is the natural world in motion, the frequency to which Bronwen Davies is aligned and where she belongs.

The rules are simple and everlasting, and the sun sets the pace.

Jacqueline Jones, *Rhondda Street Youths*

He Only Swore in Welsh

By Tony Webb

Jacqueline Jones, *Unemployed Man*

I grew up with my grandfather. Well, that is how it seemed. He only lived a few hundred yards away, and I swear that on sunny days I could see the sun shining on his bald head, as he worked in his garden. His name was Ernest, but I called him 'Dad Ern'.

Ern was a Communist. He'd worked in Aber Tin Works in Swansea during the years of industrial unrest in the 1920s and 1930s. He had been blacklisted from other jobs. He had also been offered foreman positions if he gave up his Trade Union activities. He refused, and probably not politely.

In his later years he had worked for the Electricity Board. When he retired he put his framed retirement testimonial under his bed, next to the pisspot.

We all lived in a village called Pentre-dwr, known throughout Swansea as 'little Moscow.' This was because just about every man in the village was a 'red.' Most houses took *The Daily Worker* newspaper. Ern was well known and respected as one of the oldest and founder members of the Swansea Communist Party. Academics and students with left wing sympathies made pilgrimages from Swansea University to seek out his views on recent events and also to collect his contribution to Party funds. Sometimes the conversations would not go the way they expected, especially if they criticised Russia.

'Of course,' they challenged, 'Hungary was a mistake, and Czechoslovakia too!'

A short silence, then a detailed response from Dad Ern. 'CIA orchestrated,' he said. 'Those uprisings were designed to bring down Moscow and destabilise the east.'

From a drawer he brought out a faded pamphlet.

'All predicted, all expected by Lenin. Read this,' he said.

The academics and their acolytes were out of their depth. All their arguments were countered by quotations from Marx. They rose from their seats, sometimes up to half a dozen of then, and moved slowly backwards towards the door and then through the gate, back to their burrows in Derwen Fawr and Mumbles. Sometimes he followed them to the gate, quoting dialectical materialism.

Every day, except Sunday, he read the *Daily Worker*, and on Friday the *Soviet Weekly*, with its boasts of wheat production in the Ukraine and how many tractors had been built in the Soviet Union the previous year. My cousin, Kev, whose father also bought the Soviet Weekly, agreed with me that it was the most boring publication we'd ever seen.

My head, however, was always in 'The Valiant' comic, which my Uncle Huw brought me from Swansea Market on Saturdays. Dad Ern would spot these comics from twenty yards. I knew what was coming next:

'Imperialist propaganda! Pithing the minds of the young. Preparing the youth of today for the next war, glorifying violence and bloodshed.'

This was not said in a cruel way, but almost sympathetically. Boys' comics in the 1960s were indeed quite violent, with the Japanese and Germans being given a right hammering every week. The stories were illustrated with vicious graphics; the 'Japs' and the 'Krauts' being blown to bits in colour on the front pages and in black and white on the inside. I was used to Dad Erns' misgivings, but I read on.

Ern had many virtues and, to me, not many faults. And he only swore in Welsh! And he never smacked me; not once; ever.

Only twice during my entire childhood did he lose his temper with me. Once when Hadyn, a slightly older lad, and I sat on the dry stone wall at the bottom of Ern's garden, and leisurely, with our sandaled feet, kicked brick after brick into the field next door. We didn't mean any harm. Nippers doing what bored nippers do during the summer holidays. The wall had to be rebuilt by Ern and Uncle Huw, stone by stone.

A few days later my mother said, 'Your grandfather isn't very happy with you.' I kept away for about four days. He never mentioned it, though. I was ashamed. He forgave me; he always did.

The second time trouble occurred was when I painted the piano blue. My grandmother, Dinah, had gone out shopping. Ern was in the greenhouse with his tomatoes. When he came in for his tea, there was blue paint everywhere. I'd seen the tin in the cellar and had enthusiastically got to work. Paint on the carpet, paint on my hands and trousers, and most of the piano a shade of sky blue.

He said something in Welsh. 'Beth uffarn mae'r crotyn gwneud nawr!' The literal translation into English is quite mild. 'What the hell is the boy doing now?' Not particularly frightening in English, but, take it from me, when boomed out in Welsh, it is more devastating than ten bas...s!

He looked at me and I heard him mutter, 'Jawl!', 'Devil' in English, but, once again, in Welsh a right rollicking, especially when you are only ten. I scarpered. Things must have been bad.

Later on in my twenties, I did not need any reminders that he had not mellowed, particularly his politics, and his opinion of America.

From 1974 until 1980 we lived together in the same house. Now a widower, he spent most of his time in the garden. Once a week he'd go to the local pub at about nine o'clock, after much debating as to whether he needed a shave or not. He'd come home at about twenty past eleven, and God help me if I was watching anything 'Yankee' on the television. I'd hear his key in the door and his winter breath would come in with the night air. He'd pick up on the accent on the television.

'Yanks!' he'd say, 'Load of crooks and anti-Union gangsters. Warmongers!'

I would switch off the television and make for the stairs. I knew he was right.

He still is.

Chartist Memorial, Newport
Photograph courtesy of Hugh Thomas

Struggle on the Wall

By Phil Knight

The real problem with these statues of racist bastards is that they have stood so long. Lording it over our public space like gods of the ancient world (which was of course the inspiration). The real question is why have they stood so long? In parts of Britain, we have had Labour Party control of Local government for almost a hundred years. So why do they still stand?

As a reformist party committed to 'the parliamentary road to Socialism', the Labour Party believes it can manage the state in the interest of all classes. These statues of 'great' men (they are almost always men) were heroes of the capitalist state in war or commerce. And reformist ideology places the state and its marble and bronze heroes above class. So, they stayed put for centuries.

It is particularly galling when Labour councillors almost fall over themselves to destroy working-class memorials in the interests of the free market. An infuriating example was when Newport Labour Council in South Wales destroyed the beautiful Chartist mural by Kenneth Budd in October 2013 in order to build a new 'shopping experience'. The was a wonderful celebration of the Chartist Uprising of 1839. When workers fought and died to win the right to vote. The mural was on a wire framework and could have easily been preserved and transferred to a museum. Indeed, the late Mr Budd's family offered to do just that. But the council destroyed it with jackhammers and the bits were thrown into a rubbish skip.

After public outrage, the Council replaced the mural with The Chartist Steps. So now you can walk all over the People's Charter. Honestly you cannot make this shit up. It is beyond satire.

If local authorities are wise, they will remove these statues of slavers, racists, war criminals and other monsters. Maybe they could be collected and displayed in context in a sort of Hall of Shame or a Museum of the Damned.

Carnival of Change

By Caroline Richards

Once upon a time Nature chose a spinning blue jewel on which to grow. Immaculately set within the Milky Way deep in the rich velvet folds of the cosmos, life became abundant, and the jewel became precious. Naturally, the flora and fauna included humans. Perhaps less naturally, the minds of some began to detach from the mother that spawned them. Humans—not exclusively but including those living on the western half of the tectonic plate known as Europe— developed senses of identity...

A few millennia on, the more needy identities became known as egos. The era of ego spread via testosterone through subsequent generations of humans - often fair skinned and mostly identifying as male. As the number of humans swelled, each ego struggled harder to be seen, to find their identity- until the strength of their numbers alone shook the fine balance of Earth's surface; undermined its crust and scagged its atmospheric gossamer veil with daily trails. The more the human numbers grew, the more they strived and detached from Mother Nature. Egos warped and realigned as controllers rather than partakers. The stronger their constructs became the more they failed their siblings. Constructs of money destroyed the balance of nature and time-honoured habits, and habitats were ripped up with bulldozers of death. Unrestrained events snowballed until the poles lost their permafrost and the oceans their reefs ...and when the self-written, filmed and directed final episode of The Age of Homo Sapiens sat within sight on the horizon, Planet Earth played a card that she keeps up its sleeve for occasions such as these... she played the species-getting-out-of-hand virus card. Humanoid governments hit panic mode and for one third of humankind's population, lockdown did ensue.

And the winds of change blew through unsettlingly, powerfully— regardless of society's expectancies, Swaddling those self-proclaimed wise men in swathes of the unknown ...

shrouded and clouded.
Like magnificently untamed demigods the winds eddied and swirled
and blustered and hurled
through cities and minds
Bombastic, fantastic and utterly... unprecedented
And so the carnival of change threw a curve ball through the portals of
time and stopped those humans on their doom-ridden tracks.
Humanoids in limbo with choices
whose voices will they hear,
their own? ... or their Mother's.

Osian Grifford, *Rhondda Floods*

Clyw Lais Y Ddraig Yn Rhuo

Geiriau: Gwenno Dafydd   Cerddoriaeth: Katherine Cole

(Clyw lais y ddraig yn rhuo x2)
Wrth lannau'r Taf
R'oedd lleisiau mil yn sisial
Ac i Gaernarfon
Bu siglo muriau'r mawrion
Ar waed y llechi
Daeth llechen lan y cyffro
A Cymru newydd
Sydd nawr ar fin dihuno.
(Clyw lais y ddraig yn rhuo x2)

Pum mil a mwy
I Ferthyr ddaeth o bobman
O'r De i'r Gogledd
O Amlwch i Rydaman
Yn Sgwar Penderyn
Cartref ein cyndeidiau
Mae'r gwreichion gwan
Yn prysur dyfu'n fflamau
Daw, Cymru yn rhydd.

Cytgan
Paid digalonni
A paid a bod yn brudd
R'ol tlodi a dioddef.
Daw Cymru eto'n rhydd.
Dim plygu clun
Daw pawb yn un.
A'r ddraig sydd ar ddihun.
(Clyw lais y ddraig yn rhuo x2)

Mae'r clymau caeth
Yn brysur ddatgymalu
Ein lleisiau croch yn
Atseinio o Fon i Fynwy
Daeth tro ar fyd
Ag agor mae'r llifddorau
Mae ysbryd Lewsyn
Yn berwi'n ein gwithiennau.
Daw, Cymru yn rhydd.

Cytgan
Paid digalonni a paid a bod yn brudd
R'ol tlodi a dioddef.
Daw Cymru eto'n rhydd.
Dim plygu clun
Daw pawb yn un
A'r ddraig sydd ar ddihun.
Rhan olaf—Semitone i fynu
(Clyw lais y ddraig yn rhuo)
Mae sibrwd uwch y llynnoedd
(Clyw lais y ddraig yn rhuo)
A chorau yn y cymoedd
(Clyw lais y ddraig yn rhuo)
Mae'r sain yn tyfu dros ein tir
(Clyw lais y ddraig yn rhuo)
Daw Annibyniaeth cyn bo hir.

Photograph courtesy of Mike Jenkins

Hear Sound of Dragons Roaring

Song by Gwenno Dafydd

Hear sound of dragons roaring. Hear sound of dragons roaring. (BV)
    Along the Taff
    A thousand voices murmured
    And in Caernarfon
    The ancient ramparts shuddered
    A new beginning
    Was on the verge of breaking
    A mighty Wales
    Was finally awaking.
Hear sound of dragons roaring. Hear sound of dragons roaring. (BV)
Five thousand came to Merthyr in the morning
    Journeys begun
    Before the day was dawning
    Penderyn Square home
    Of our brave fore-fathers
    Hear voices loud now
    Of brothers, sisters, mothers.
    Wales rise and be free.
Chorus
    Don't be downhearted
    There's no need to be sad
    All marching 'neath one banner
    Be joyous and be glad
    Our time is coming
    We've broken down the door
    And prisoners we no more.
Hear sound of dragons roaring. Hear sound of dragons roaring.
    The chains that bind
    Are finally being broken
    The words long lost
    Are proudly being spoken.

The tide has turned
The circle how completed
The ruling classes
At last will be defeated.
Wales rise and be free.

Chorus

Last part

Hear sound of dragons roaring
Hear whispers in the alleys
Hear sound of dragons roaring
Commotion in the valleys
Hear sound of dragons roaring.
Let's all reclaim our powers
Hear sound of dragons roaring.
And Independence will be ours.

Kizzy & Eady Crawford singing at the Merthyr March, courtesy of Mike Jenkins

Is it time for Our Nation's Artists, Poets, Actors, Musicians, and Authors to get stuck into Political Activism?

Biographer, Leon Noakes talks with Super Furry Animals' Cian Ciaran

Photograph courtesy of Taz Rahman

Leon Noakes, author of *Withdrawn Traces: Searching for the Truth About Richey Manic* (Penguin: 2019) was one of a small handful of people who formed Yes Cymru in 2014. At those very first meetings, he found himself in the company of veteran language activists and several whose families were hard baked in the Plaid tradition. Cian Ciaran has arguably become one of the most politically outspoken musicians in Wales, and currently sits on the Executive Committee of Yes Cymru. He was invited to share his views on Welsh politics and the role of cultural figures.

Thinking back, the Super Furry Animals were surely in the mix of thoughts, feelings and events that led to my becoming involved the Welsh independence movement. No-one I knew had ever voted for Plaid Cymru, but in the context of the rise of New Labour, the realisation dawned that the kind of society we needed would never be achieved under Westminster rule. UK institutions inherited the imperial tradition of governing vast areas of the globe and humanity—and despite the fall of the empire, were still adept at quashing colonial natives in the British Isles.

Many frustrated voters in Valleys communities gave up the long-held tradition of automatically voting Labour and, like me, sought a home in the left-leaning flank of Plaid Cymru. Despite his markedly different background, Cian's politics fall into that tradition.

'I've always been like: it doesn't make sense to let someone else tell you what to do with your life. You haven't got an equal voice in the UK; never have, never will, because we will always have an English majority rule. That's not anti-English sentiment, that's just how it is. No-one's begrudging them that, but it's when it has a detrimental effect on Wales and the psyche. You go to the Valleys and everyone's depressed and suicidal; there's no work, no hope, and it seems like there's no end to it. That's just a cycle, and I think its manufactured. People say Wales is just an afterthought, but they have thought of us and they want to keep us poor. So, in that sense, it's the injustice, for me, not "Wales is great and ace and I love dragons and rugby!" I'm not into flag-waving nationalism. It's more like the injustice and the sense of wanting respect.'

Spoken like a true Welsh Republican! As the sole monoglot English speaker and Valleys boy, my experience in the newly formed Yes Cymru was not always comfortable, but it was one that many others would have to make if the movement was to amount to anything. It became obvious that the psychological shift would be made far easier for people through our nation's poets, musicians, actors and authors.

Potential players in the counter-hegemony, they could do more in a few short years than Plaid Cymru's politicians have done over several long decades. Winning over the people's favourite artists to the cause would go a long way to carving a channel through which the majority might then pour in. After several meetings with him and knowing the effective role Welsh musicians would then play, in 2018 I nominated Cian to the Executive Committee of Yes Cymru. Within months, such previously unlikely candidates as Charlotte Church and Goldie Lookin Chain were encouraging newcomers to the cause.

From my own perspective as a biographer of the Manic Street Preachers, the Blackwood band have leaned tantalisingly close to an endorsement. The question arises, what is it that prevents such artists from giving outright support; particularly those names who seemed already to be leaning in this direction back in the '90s?

My own turn towards Welsh patriotism came as a student of political philosophy in the mid-Nineties. But no less important for me, also in the new spirit in Welsh popular culture, in context of the 1997 vote on the creation of the Welsh Assembly. Many '90s Welsh musicians actively campaigned for the increase in autonomy, pursued by the second devolution referendum—and their impact was not insignificant. Any realistic chance of amassing a majority support for independence will inevitably rely on growing support from outside of professional politics. Once again, musicians and other cultural actors will prove indispensable. But it is never easy.

Those of us who were there, will recall the role played by Welsh musicians in the debates on devolution and the creation of the Welsh Assembly. Considering the incredibly slim 'Yes' vote in 1997, a case could be made that a generation of Welsh bands ('Cool Cymru') tipped the mood in its favour...

'At the time I didn't see it like that,' says Cian, 'I just didn't want anything to do with it. Looking back, you can see a correlation. The Super Furries were always political, but we wouldn't stay up at night on the bus talking about how we're gonna actually plan to free Wales. If anything, we liked taking the piss out of it.'

At Cian's house in Cardiff Bay, I ask him to comment on the delicate matter of other Welsh musicians—does he feel that they are naturally less political, or just more guarded?

'There's that bit of insecurity or uncertainty about who they're standing shoulder-to-shoulder with', he says, 'As in, I don't want to stand next to a fascist or racist. There is quite a lot of bravado, the macho testosterone element in the independence movement. So, it's like, do I want to be a part of that, or do I stay as a voice from the outside? But then, be the voice from outside: don't be mute! How are you going to change it? They say there's not enough women... there's a responsibility on everyone to recognise that, but how do you go about changing that? You can't do it from the outside, just criticising.'

Cian's partner Estelle (a member of the band Zefur Wolves) is present, dealing with the couple's two young sons, and steps in...

'I think it's because unless you're a Billy Bragg type person and spent your whole life doing it politically—if you're on the scale of trying to make it as a musician, people don't want to upset the press and shit like that. I don't consider myself to be someone who is gonna make money out of music, so I don't care what I say. And I am anti-establishment, but a lot of these musicians aren't really. A lot of it is an egotistical thing as well. A lot of musicians are egotistical people, and they don't want anything bruising their ego. They haven't got the balls to speak out. Let's face it, that is a part of it.'

Since 2014, Yes Cymru, has become an unavoidable force in Welsh politics, with independence now becoming a real-world option and up for serious debate. Only a few short years ago, it felt like a losing battle trying to get people to publicly advocate for Welsh independence. Those who turned out for events could fit into a bus or two, and almost all known to one another.

Most activists shouting 'Cymru Rhydd' were kept at a safe distance from a Welsh-speaking professional class, making headway in media and politics. There was a sense of a stand-off between those with the cultural confidence and ability to progress in the world of professional careers, and what they perceived as a a 'ragtag army,' the likes of whom could be seen at the annual Cilmeri gathering every December.

Working-class, Welsh patriots received short shrift from the Plaid types, who were fearful of accusations of extremism and fascism. But it was obvious that, if a new grassroots movement for Welsh independence was to grow—for the idea to become common-sensical, reasonable and mainstream —people from the professional Welsh-speaking class would be needed... it was these people who were capable of moving with ease in the new Welsh polity, to shift things up and out of a small and paranoid fringe movement. And so it proved. The resourceful confidence of this specific ingredient of Welsh society would prove very effective into putting Yes Cymru into first gear, thus steering 'indy' into the mainframe of acceptable debate.

That said, Plaid Cymru has had its leftist republican wing, offering voters an alternative to Labour. But why has Plaid been incapable of drawing forth the kind of support enjoyed by Yes Cymru?

'It's loads of things. You've got the Welsh language divide, where non-Welsh speakers and Welsh speakers are pitted against each other. You got decades of that to contend with. The idea that independence is just for the northwest Walians. People have been told that they can't vote plaid because they don't speak Welsh and who's at fault? Plaid, you could argue; if they are perceived that way then they need to work hard to undo that. Leanne [Wood] did a lot to do with that because she's a woman from the Rhondda who couldn't speak Welsh or was learning Welsh, so she was a step in the right direction. It's weird isn't it? I think, paranoia maybe... they didn't use the I-word for ten years; they tried to reinvent it in the 90s, came up with different names for it. When you think about where the SNP are now compared to Plaid—their trajectory has been phenomenal!'

A particular strain of working-class, Welsh patriotism always received short shrift from the Plaid types hellbent on professionalism and respectability, and fearful of accusations of extremism and fascism. Yes Cymru would need to tap into the patriotism of people whose main aim was not a lucrative career in the corridors of power.

In recent years, one party who has been unequivocal in its use of the I-word, has been UKIP, who shocked many by hoovering votes in the Valleys and elsewhere with a perceived revolt against the political establishment that, had they been more forthcoming, could have been Plaid's for the taking.

'Brexit itself was a protest vote. It was just anti-establishment, in the same way that they voted for Trump. In the last ten years, austerity has made people say they've had enough—but it could easily go two ways: it could either go like we're seeing [that is] right-wing, xenophobic, racist, fascist even, or we can choose another, better, healthier path. As with any movement: it's like a club or a gang and you've got a tribal mentality ... people feel comfortable, then... even if they are strangers. That's where these rallies are starting to make people come out of the closet. They feel they oppose Brexit, and don't want to be racist; that whole thing. Now there's a sense of urgency for me that wasn't there, like, five years ago. Because of Brexit and the right-wing xenophobia, not just in the UK—but everywhere. The Left are always slow to react; the only time they have ever led the charge was in Russia.'

And this is the point—the political upheaval in the Western world has "gone mad," amidst Covid-19 and the constitutional crisis in the UK—it surely is the perfect storm, providing ideal conditions for Welsh separatists to achieve what Plaid Cymru and other organisations have never managed; namely in obliging the Welsh people to confront their existential future.

'It won't be one person or one band or one figure... it's got to be a movement. Strength in numbers and all that. You need the focal point of a leader, if you like, or someone who can talk the talk and inspire, and create more leaders. There is that sense of urgency. If it doesn't happen soon, the likes of Farage are gonna get their claws in and that'll be it. That's the scary thing.'

One, perhaps, startling though encouraging remark is Cian's verdict on devolution and Welsh politics, which has transpired since the creation of the Assembly.

'Devolution doesn't mean shit', he says. 'Our hands are tied. All it's shown is that it's almost unworkable.'

But you were certainly pro-devolution back in 1997?

'Well you had to be! It's like your foot in the door—a step closer—part of normalising it... but I suppose, what it has shown is that it's not good enough. Devolution is like: "Let's keep them quiet for twenty years ... just give them a little stick and they can chew on that and argue amongst themselves. We don't have to worry about it. If they vote Yes, they'll just argue amongst each other ... we'll give them peanuts and it won't be workable." And then people will ask for it to be abolished'.

There are those on both sides wanting to scrap the current constitutional settlement, and the conscience of the nation must decide where sovereignty and allegiance are centred. The defining existential question now facing all Welsh people, is 'Cardiff or London?' Wales must rediscover its social traditions of radicalism and collectivism, in what Cornelius Castoriadis termed "the magma of social significations". In this the role artists will be crucial.

Today, We Lost Our Right to Move to 29 Countries

By Tracey Rhys

They are taking away our right to move in the land, territorial as ants warring over colonies, our movement restricted by waves seeping up our full skirts, buoying us up until saturated. Their queues are the last formation, striating rocks with their straight lines, their food banks and job queues.

We are swamped by impassable oceans. Their swells are septic, sealed with bacteria, infection insidious in our lungs. You see how we spread it around? They mention this. It multiplies even as we shrink coughing to our homes, too small and still to peer through locks. And yet... Oh, yes. I see them now.

Tracey Rhys, *Ymlaen/Onwards*

A Personal History of the Miners' Strike

By Tim Richards

The Miners' Strike of 1984-85 was a turning point in the history of Wales as the defeat of the miners marked the end of an era in our economy, society, and politics. It might seem presumptuous for me, a Further Education college law lecturer to write a personal history of the strike but I was there and became deeply involved so while this is not a definitive history, I can at least tell the story as I experienced it.

When the strike started in March 1984, I volunteered to help giving free legal advice. I advised some South Wales miners arrested for giving out leaflets against scabs in Nottingham and as the police were still finding their way about the law, they originally charged them with giving out obscene publications! I joke not—that is how the police worked from start to finish— arrest first and find reasons later.

The 1972 and 1974 miners' strikes had taught the Tories and the miners the same lesson—starve the country of coal and the miners would win but the Tories were better prepared. When the miners on strike found that they could get no benefits and that the union had no money to help them they faced starvation and rapid defeat before they even started. Unfortunately, in April 1984, this was only just being fully realised by the S. Wales NUM.

It was while I was giving legal advice in their Pontypridd HQ that Kim Howells, their researcher, explained the desperate need for support groups to feed the miners' families and that is how I came to set up the Rhymney Valley Miners Support Group (RVMSG) As a political activist who had helped the Nantgarw Coking Ovens NUM lodge in their campaign against its closure by Labour in 1978 and had addressed NUM lodges on the threat posed by Thatcher's nuclear power programme before the strike, I had contacts and called the first meeting in Caerphilly Workmen's Hall.

It was one of the first miners support groups to get organised and it was one of the largest as it covered the NUM lodges of Nantgarw/ Windsor and Nantgarw Coking ovens, Caerphilly tar plant, Bedwas and Penallta. Because we were ahead of the S.Wales NUM we did not fit their plans so we were added, arbitrarily, to the Gwent Food fund, even though we were largely outside Gwent. I took the media a while to catch up too and at our third meeting a BBC news team turned up to film it and I agreed but only if they paid us. I am still awaiting the cheque.

Early on in the strike we got hold of a newsletter produced by the Dulais Valley Miners Support Group and we decide to produce our own weekly newsletter "Rhymney Valley Report" which had a print run of 3-4,000 and was distributed outside the valley because there was nothing else in our area. As the support for the miners grew, one of the earliest developments were the local Miners Wives Support Groups that sprung up and which we supported as they developed into wider activities beyond food collection and distribution to joining the picket lines.

My whole life outside work revolved around the strike. We held meetings on Sundays, either in Penyrheol or Bedwas, and I would then type up our weekly newsletter, the Rhymney Valley Report (RVR) on my BBC B computer, print it on a dot matrix printer, add pictures and written headlines and hand it over to Lyn the printer in the Rhymney Valley District Council (RVDC) where I would pick it up on a Wednesday for distribution on Thursdays. Then I was out collecting food and money over the weekend in the streets and going round the houses. In my village of Abertridwr, as throughout the South Wales valleys, the response to our collections was overwhelmingly supportive even though the number of miners actually working was tiny in comparison to the population. Some memories remain vivid—like the time I called on a young couple with a baby in a rather bare terraced house near where I lived and they invited me into a largely empty kitchen with no food around who rummaged around in their cupboard to find some tins of food for us. I felt humbled by their spirit of support and if the miners could have survived on that alone then they would still be out on strike today.

We began the Summer with a demonstration, organising marches from Abertridwr, Ystrad Mynach and Bedwas, (representing the local NUM lodges) to Caerffili where they joined to march round the town to Morgan Jones Park for a public meeting. We managed to co-ordinate the marches meeting up by having leaders of each march in touch with me, on the Abertridwr march, using local CB enthusiasts. It took a lot of organising to get it right but I was as pleased as punch when they all met up smoothly at the Piccadilly crossroads.

Politics in the area was dominated by Labour and Plaid Cymru and their active members support was crucial. I believe that being a Welsh socialist in neither party explains why I was chosen to be Chairperson of the Miners Support Group and helped me to chair meetings in a fair way that was acceptable to both sides.

Being a large group had its advantages, as when, in the Summer of 1984, George Melly offered to do some fund-raising concerts. We hosted one of them in the Aneurin Labour club in Penyrheol and this was one of the strike's high moments. When George Melly did his concert, he introduced himself by saying "'DIS OLE STRIKE'S GONNA GET IT SOME STYLE'". He was living in Brecon and his wife Diane organised his mini-tour and George loved the audience of miners and their families as much as they loved him. It was at this concert that I first heard the newly formed Côr Cochion Caerdydd, the Cardiff Red Choir, which is still going.

One of the high points of the strike for me happened at a fund-raising event in Pontlottyn when I was introduced to Will Paynter, the legendary NUM and Communist leader who was 81 but looked, walked, talked, and thought 20 years younger. Miners of his generation had fought the battles of the General Strike and the 1930s and it was a battle repeated during 1984-85 when the miners once again faced the full aggressive power of the British state represented by the police who had learnt the lessons of the flying pickets of the 1972 and 1974 strikes.

Although I attended a couple of pickets, I mainly got to know about how the strike was being policed through working for the Welsh Campaign for Civil and Political Liberty inquiry into the policing of the miners' strike which led to the report *Striking Back*. I interviewed dozens of miners from local lodges about the way in which the police were using their powers to restrict the miners picketing and it was obvious from the start that the miners were not going to be allowed to put their arguments to those crossing their picket lines as the police used obstruction of the highway to prevent it. It was a simple legal argument that they used—once a miner had stopped a car or lorry to talk to the driver they were obstructing the highway. Soon the police started to stop pickets miles away from the picket line, usually by threatening the drivers, a practice later ruled to be unlawful. After that it became farcical as the miners were even told that they could not shout "scab" at the scabs. One interview I did was in the NUM office in Crumlin which was under siege, occupied by miners to stop it being seized by the courts under a Sequestration order because the strike had been declared illegal and the assets of the NUM were threatened.

But it was the experience of Orgreave that really taught the miners what they were facing—the raw force of the new paramilitary tactics developed by the police. Their suspicions were aroused when they got there as instead of being obstructive the police actually told them where to park. As one miner told me "There was no doubt about it—it was an exercise aimed at giving us a real pasting". This was a view supported years later by ex-Chief Constable Alderson, of Devon and Cornwall in a documentary about Orgreave. Looking at the police's own video he concluded that the trouble was actually started by the police. Nothing has changed as similar aggression was used by the police in the Climate Change demo in recent years and another similarity was the fact that many police officers during the Miners' Strike displayed no numbers which, of course, makes them more difficult to identify. The miners were capable of direct action themselves and I well remember a couple of our group who were in high spirits at one meeting as they had managed to sabotage a train load of coal by opening the doors on the railway trucks to pour the loads onto the line.

As the strike wore on, the issue of scabbing became important as other areas, like North Wales, drifted back to work and became scabs, tempted by a bonus bribe from the NCB. Our response was to increase the venom we poured on them and several issues of the weekly newsletter concentrated on this, with cartoons such as the "Anatomy of a Scab" with an explanation of his gormless head—"Eyes—can't see what he is doing. Nose—can't smell himself. Ears—listens to what he wants to hear. Mouth—always open, giving excuses. Brain—the only part not working".

It was in this climate of frustration and anger that the miners reacted to the first scabbing in South Wales, and this led to the tragic killing of a Cardiff taxi driver David Wilkie, on the Heads of the Valley road near Rhymney in December 1984 when two miners Dean Hancock and Russell Shankland dropped a concrete block into the path of a taxi taking a scab to work.

When they were convicted of murder the reaction in the valley was shock as we believed that they had not intended to kill anyone and that became the key issue in the case which was finally resolved long after the strike had finished.

When the House of Lords dismissed the murder charge, they replaced it with manslaughter and issued guidelines for future juries in a sensible and clear precedent which asks a jury to assess first the likelihood of an act leading to death and then consider whether, as a result, it might have been foreseen and therefore intended.

When we had to go out collecting soon after the accident, we were not sure how people would react but we should not have worried and the Christmas spirit lifted us when we went carol singing. It was a hard time and one episode is particularly telling. Some miners had seen what the Gwent Food Fund had planned for the meagre Christmas meal and not unreasonably they argued that the RVMSG had raised large sums of money while other areas were not as well-organised and that we should keep back some of the cash we had raised to buy something extra for our local families. After a heated debate it was decided that we should not do that as everyone should get the same. Although no-one said it, this was a practical application of the Marx's principle for Communism, "From each according to their ability, to each according to their needs."

The miners' political consciousness was broad and it was no surprise to me that a number of them joined an anti-Nuclear power demonstration at Hinkley Point in Somerset on weekend despite the fact that they got no travel expenses. On the other hand, that politics also engendered wonderful camaraderie as we supported a group of isolated striking miners in Nottinghamshire who were ostracised by their local community of scabs in a mirror image of our experience. The stresses and strains of staying out on strike created huge problems and tensions in marriages which inevitably led, sometimes, to bitterness and divorce and the children of the miners were often damaged too.

The South Wales miners had been slow in joining the strike partly because of resentment that they had not been supported in their call for support against pit closures in the valleys in late 1983. It was a considered and realistic view of many South Wales miners that the strike had come too late, that starting a strike in March was stupid because the demand for coal dropped after the winter and it would take longer to starve the country of coal. But when the strike started in earnest, South Wales joined with a vengeance and maintained a 99% turnout, more than any other area, until it finished.

The end of the strike came fast and the straw that broke the camel's back happened when Kim Howells spoke to the Media about the return to work. Why a lowly, unelected researcher for the S.Wales NUM was the main spokesman was, and still is, a mystery, but many of us noted his rapid elevation to become Labour MP for Pontypridd and the questions remain, many years on.

As Arthur Scargill had predicted, and we had always known would happen, Margaret Thatcher then closed down the coal-mining industry including a handful of pits in South Wales which were still profitable, the proof of which was evidenced by the success of Tower colliery bought and run by the miners for a decade after. But revenge was not long in coming as the Anti-Poll Tax campaign of the early 90s saw many of the same people fighting back and winning, but that is another story.

Alan Perry, *'How far down?'*

Immigrants Built Merthyr

By Gerhard Kress

Photograph courtesy of Gerhard Kress

I was surrounded, friends across the road, beside me, behind me and sitting in the middle of the road. Standing, looking serious, talking into communication devices, men of the Police, trying to square the circle. Eventually herding 'Remainers' into the gated Trago Mills concentration compound of 'Leavers.' Many others had impatiently turned their cars and scarpered. The French Huguenot who had woefully failed to secure himself a German passport was about to address the ten thousand supporters who turned out to be 133 white, middle-aged, insecure men. On course to complete where Oswald Mosley had left off decades earlier.

Both had chosen a town built by immigrants to rail against immigration.

There he was, inside his car, in front of the young couple sitting on hard tarmac. He was staring at me. Visibly fuming, one stretched "stick it up your arse" middle-finger. His eyes burning into mine. And that's when he said it.

I have childhood memories after Germany had finally been liberated from the tyranny of fascism. But fascism had not disappeared, had gone into temporary visible hiding. Middle-aged German men saying it in pubs, on the street and unashamedly.

Adolf never knew about concentration camps.

Adolf never ordered them.

Adolf would've known how to deal with the likes of you. Long-haired feminized hippies.

And, if you don't like it here, and, if you don't shut the fuck up, why then don't you go over the wall, to your East German communist comrades.

That man with his middle finger sticking up. His eyes, pure venom. His voice: "Go back home to Germany!"

My friends know how that feels. They've known for a long time. They've known from playgrounds, school and workplaces. Nothing more than the colour of their skin had made them targets. My son had experienced it in school: "Nazi" or "Jew Boy", often in the same sentence. And if they wanted to be, what they thought of as really hurtful, they'd call him "English" or worse, "Cardiff".

I am taking an endless stream of photographs, recording Merthyr Tydfil dealing with fascism. Just as they did when Oswald Mosley marched his Blackshirts into their town. I am doing what I have always done, making a record for future students of history to discover in the library's historical rummage shoe box.

Moments later, emulating Mahatma Gandhi's peaceful resistance, Jamie is being picked up and off the street. Clothing in disarray when police hands arrest and place him inside a police van for incarceration and interrogation. I watch, I photograph, and I am admiring his quiet dignity.

Within minutes, a muscular, heavy-set man runs up to a woman on the opposite pavement. She is holding a small child in her arms. Momentarily paralyzed, I watch as his fists are about to smash into her face. Private security guards, now nationally more numerous than the police, guarding those who can afford to pay for their services, just as they can afford to pay for their health privately and undermine the NHS. It's the guards who are upon him a fraction before his fists can smash into the face of woman and toddler. It takes four to restrain this raging bull. He is not arrested for attempted violence. He is not being charged, not being cautioned, details are not taken.

Instead, violence is given a pat on the back and send off into the compound to listen to Farage's speech of hatred.

The peaceful voice against fascism is bundled into a police van, spending the night in jail, and ordered to pay a fine.

So ... why don't I just do as that man says, "Go home to Germany?" together with 3.3 million other unwanted aliens from all European countries. And who can count the Belgians who made their home in Italy, the Welsh living in England, the English and their second homes in Cornwall and all those people settled in Spain and those who thought they'd never leave the USA, Canada, or Australia again.

We are all immigrants, just as we all 'belong'.

Two years ago, in front of BBC and ITV cameras and in the National Assembly of Wales and in the committee room and in the lobby of the House of Commons I was quite certain.

"I live here, this is my home. Home of my family, where my friends live. Where I've lived, loved and worked for most of my life."

When my country went into temporary, collective insanity over the war of an island off the coast of South America. And again, when my emotionally buttoned-up country drifted on a wave of emotions over the death of a young woman of the ruling class. A woman whose persona had been invented by the media to sell newspapers, teddy bears, toilet rolls and airwave viewing time. And finally, when a badly conducted opinion poll, manipulated with criminal intent, managed to hold up a mirror, showing us who we really are.

Badly educated, badly informed in an educational apartheid system, controlled by those few on the other side. Holding on to a perverted view of history that never was. Idolizing our rape of the world. And demonstrating that the UNITED Kingdom has a precarious hold on its unity.

What's left is just one question, 'What is home?' I thought I knew the answer.

Photograph courtesy of Gerhard Kress

Imam Sis, Day 90 of Hunger Strike:
Message On UN International Anti-Racism Day 2019

Introduced by Adam Johannes, Secretary, Cardiff Stop the War Coalition

Photograph courtesy of Taz Rahman

The hunger strike of Imam Sis, a Kurdish activist living in South Wales was a milestone in Welsh history—and the longest known hunger strike in British history. Between December 17 2018 and May 26 2019 basing himself at the Kurdish Community Centre in Newport he survived for almost six months living on nothing but water, a daily glass of homemade lemonade, B1 & B12 vitamin tablets and a tiny amount of sugar and salt. While this prolonged the hunger strike it was a serious action which his friends, including me, feared might end in death.

The action was undertaken to support Leyla Guven, a mother and socialist-feminist MP in the Turkish Parliament whose hunger strike sparked over 7000 Kurds around the world to join her on hunger strike and call for an end to the isolation of Kurdish leader, Abdullah Ocalan. Imprisoned since 1999, mostly in solitary confinement, he is widely recognised by friend and foe alike as central to any peaceful resolution of the Kurdish question in Turkey.

In March 2019, following a motion tabled by Plaid Cymru, Wales became the first parliament in the world to show to show solidarity with Kurdish hunger strikers and the then Labour leader Jeremy Corbyn met with Welsh Kurdish community members joining their call for Öcalan to be allowed access to his lawyers. Imam's action attracted widespread solidarity from the Welsh political and cultural scene, and considerably raised the profile of the Kurdish issue in Wales.

The following statement was issued on UN Anti-Racism Day, which commemorates the anniversary of the Sharpeville massacre in apartheid South Africa, in support of hundreds marching against racism through Cardiff, capital of Wales.

We strongly condemn the racist attack targeting two mosques in Christchurch, New Zealand, a city with a strong Muslim population. We pray for those who lost their lives and extend our condolences to the families of the victims, to all Muslims and the people of New Zealand and wish a speedy recovery to the wounded.

This attack is another sign of the clear and present danger posed by racism and hate speech to the world today. This attack is a result of the discrimination imposed by the ruling powers of the world, and it is not only a social but also a political problem. And the solution to this problem is to raise the struggle for democracy against the type of mentality that discriminates between communities, beliefs, languages, cultures and identities, and spreads hate speech.

We want you to know that as a people struggling in Kurdistan and in many other parts of the world together with our comrades from other communities, our struggle has only one single goal—to paraphrase what one of the most beloved singers among the Kurds, the Armenian artist Aram Tigran, said: to melt all the tanks, guns and weapons in the world and turn them into music instruments.

We want to thank you for providing us, as the Kurdish community, with the opportunity to stand together with you, shoulder to shoulder, on this important day accepted by the UN as a day to eliminate all kinds of racism.

Comrades, March 21 is seen as the international day to eliminate racism. For us, as the Kurdish people, March 21 marks the end of the deadly cold of winter, the re-awakening and revival of nature, the beginning of a new year. On this day, we celebrate Newroz, which symbolizes the people's liberation struggle against bloodthirsty, oppressive tyrants, it signifies the resistance started by Kawa the Blacksmith, who ignited the fire of rebellion in the mountains of Kurdistan.

The Kurdish people have historically experienced brutal massacres and wars in the month of March. On March 16, 1988, the racist dictator Saddam Hussein murdered 5,000 Kurds, mostly women and children, in Halabja within hours, using chemicals that he obtained from Western states. Last year on March 18, 2018, the racist dictator of the Turkish state, Recep Tayyip Erdogan and jihadist mercenary gangs occupied the northern Syrian city of Afrin, where the different communities had been living together in a fraternal and peaceful manner. While thousands of civilians were massacred with the help of combat jets and tanks sold to the Turkish army by Britain and Germany, hundreds of thousands of people were forcibly displaced in this attempted genocide against the Kurds through planned ethnic cleansing and demographic change. While honouring and commemorating those, who have lost their lives in these wars, we want to once again renew our promise to collectively struggle for a world without war and exploitation.

Dear comrades, dear friends,

Once again, we want to remind you that while the Kurdish people have been struggling between life and death for decades against the racist states of Turkey, Iran, Iraq and Syria, who have denied and assaulted the Kurds' identity, language and culture, a socialist women's revolution developed in Rojava as a result of this struggle and as living proof that the era of revolutions is far from being over.

The political and ideological leader of this revolution, which is based on the solidarity of peoples, women's liberation, peace, pluralism and democracy, is the PKK leader Abdullah Öcalan, imprisoned for 20 years on Imrali Prison Island by the Turkish state. In violation of his basic human rights, the Turkish state is currently imposing a brutal isolation regime on him. Since 2011, he has not been allowed to meet with his lawyers. For years, he has been isolated from the outside world, including his own family, although he plays a historic role for peace and reconciliation in Turkey, Kurdistan and the Middle East.

For this reason, to put an end to the isolation, Leyla Güven MP of the Peoples' Democratic Party (HDP) started an indefinite and irreversible hunger strike 129 days ago, on November 8, 2018. This form of action spread to the prisons in Kurdistan and Turkey and then to Europe and other parts of the world. In Newport, our comrade Imam Sis continues his hunger strike on the 90th day. Although many of the hunger strikers are dangerously approaching death, the European Council and its Committee for the Prevention of Torture— the CPT—, are not taking any steps whatsoever. European governments, above all the British and German states, are either directly supporting the Turkish state's racist and fascist policies or become complicit in this injustice through their calculated silence.

Dear comrades, finally, we want to say this: if the nationalist, racist, sexist states of this capitalist and imperialist system provide each other with all sorts of support, we, as the peoples of the world, must be able to put our differences and ideological discussions aside to struggle alongside each other and to stand beside one another in solidarity and support. In this sense, we salute all people, communities, and groups at this rally with our deepest revolutionary feelings and love. We wish that you help put pressure on the Council of Europe and the CPT in support of the hunger strikers' demands—before it's too late.

With revolutionary salutes and respect,
Wales Democratic Kurdish People's Assembly.

Am I Black Enough?

By Kate Cleaver

The actor Chadwick Boseman died recently. I didn't know him, no more than anyone else. He leapt across my TV screen in black with cat ears and claws, and I have to say I thought he was one well-made man. He first hit my radar when he thanked Denzel Washington for paying for him to go through theatre school. I remember thinking that he must be a really good guy. I looked on, bemused as there was an outcry that *Black Panther* only had three white people in it. I hadn't noticed. I saw him as a nice guy, but the world saw him as a black man making good. Yes, he was black, but did that make him any better than anyone else? His modesty and kindness set him apart for me. Did you know he gave away his MTV award to an African American who had stopped a gunman?

All week I have been battling with a white suprem acist on my Facebook feed, saying that black people will get shot until they learn to obey the rules; that all the black guys killed were evil or paedophiles. That to be black is to be bad. Black is bad. Coloured is bad. White people are not bad, just misunderstood. All week and longer this kind of abuse has scrolled past me, leaving me asking myself: why am I this person's friend?

Well, I could insulate myself from people like this, but that would give me a bubble perspective. I would start to think that the world was like how I make my home: safe and free from prejudice. But it just isn't like that! Yes, it is distressing to read what someone who doesn't see themselves as racist but is an 'All Lives Matter' follower thinks. By allowing them on my friends list, provides me with a fundamental, albeit distressing perspective, that is needed in the fight against racism.

When I was younger my granddad asked me what was worrying me. We didn't know at the time I was autistic, but I had problems understanding feelings. I asked Grandad how do you know if you are happy? "Well," he said, "if you are content then you are happy." I thought about that a moment. "So, I'm happy?" He went silent. He knew about the bullying. "You understand sadness?"

"Yes," I said, "you cry."

"Well, happiness is the opposite of that. You can't feel real happiness without real sadness. One allows the other to be felt." (That was my Granddad trying to explain feelings). I then began to understand the reasons why I allow myself to be hurt, why I trust everyone and why I have white supremacists on my Facebook feed. And I read what they share and write, because to isolate myself in a bubble of comfort and safety would be a lie. One I could maintain by only exposing myself to certain people and experiences, but I refuse to limit my life. If the person I meet in the pub once a month is a white supremacist and I know it, then I can arm myself. But what has come as a shock is that those same people, those white supremacists who have been sharing posts about Boseman; how it's "such a loss", "a tragedy", "how he will be missed", makes my skin crawl. It is hypocrisy at its worst. It is this that makes me sad because they do not understand the duality of their thoughts. That can't see their own racism. That is white privilege.

I can take the rough with the smooth.

I have faced the police, to be told that the man who attacked me was a war hero, and they would not pursue him in a court. That he was very *sorry* about the wounds he inflicted, and he was seeking *help* and had been given *help* for his post-traumatic stress disorder.

I watched those exact same police officers walk out of the room and choose not to see the blood that poured from my wounds.

Where was my help? Where was my justice?

After all, I was nothing more than, well, me. And my Anglo-Indian female description couldn't match his hero status. He was a veteran. But at the same time, that awful experience left a legacy of emotional and physical scars that have haunted me for years after the attack. Where was my help? I may not have fought in his war, but my day-to-day life sometimes felt like a warzone.

I was in a restaurant and asked for the wine list. The waiter, who was no more than a boy, left and came back. "Red, white and rose". That was all he said. Even today he makes me smile. I was sat opposite the devil, an abusive, yet heroic man filled with conflict that showed on his hands, and I laughed with him, once the waiter had left. I think what happened makes that moment of normality more human than anything that happened after. The man who had left scars that still have not healed, and yet I laughed. Even in times of fear and pain, I laughed. That is the moment that keeps me sane.

Now we all know that black lives matter. We all know about systemic racism, even if some choose to refute it or ignore it. Would my life have been different if I had experienced the attack now? Maybe. Would the police have listened when I said it was more about grooming and financial dominance than the physical attack? Maybe. I still laughed though. We laughed. Even the most evil people are still people. Even those white supremacists on my news feed are people. They are scared. But I know that in all cases we can laugh together. You see, I know everyone on my Facebook feed. I have either face-timed them, phoned them or met them in person. It is only because of black lives matter that their true colours have come through. I can see them fully. Otherwise, the side they'd have showed me would have been what I wanted me to see.

But one aspect, that I hadn't realised, and would become apparent, is my fear of being black enough. My name is English, and I live a very British life. Sure, I can cook curry but then so can anyone who follows recipes. And my favourite meal is still roast lamb with all the trimmings.

I recently had a meeting with a creative writer looking for Indian people to help tell stories. He was white. He told me of a troupe he was talking to in India and how they were working together and how they were very small in numbers. How they were an inspiration. And all the time I could tell he was taking my dress in; my *Doctor Who* T-shirt and hair scraped back in a bun. The silver chain at my neck and the mug of tea in my hands. He saw something he didn't expect. And although he told me my stories may not match what they were looking for, it was clear from his face that he was disappointed. I was speaking to a friend afterwards and I said that I wondered if I'd worn my wedding sari to the meeting then would things have been different? Would I fit the stereotype he was looking for?

"What do you mean?" they asked.

"Well, you know I was on crutches for the wedding?" (I had fallen and tore a ligament in my knee only days before while on my hen night). "Yes," they said.

You can't wear a sari and be on crutches at the same time, so I had to wear the back-up dress.

"If I'd done that meeting in a sari, I may have been black enough."

My friend was shocked that I had thought I wasn't black enough. But it was bound to happen, for someone not black, the concept of having an identity determined by skin is alien. Yet that identity can be stripped from you because you are not enough. I am, to all intents and purposes, living a 'white' life with a few Indian add-ons, and none of those are the big things. My dress is mostly *white*, my name is *white*, my education is *white*, and I consider myself a lapsed Catholic! For a lot of well-meaning people, I am just not 'black enough' to readdress the balance. The odd thing is that I will be hit with being 'ethnic' and at the same time I seem to be left on the side because I'm just not *ethnic* enough. I could live in a bubble that means I don't have to cope with this. I could hide behind my husband and not expose myself to any of it. But I choose to laugh, and write, to poke fun at the situation and make others laugh, and get them to think about what they are laughing at, despite the thoughts of others and those trying to make their own privileged mistakes and omissions. And there may only be red, white, and rose on the wine list, but they are all made from grapes. Until people can understand that people like me, and others, will always be on the outskirts of society, and one type of person or another will always have privilege.

Photograph courtesy of Taz Rahman

Black Lives Matter Speech

By Neelufur Adam (Nelly Adam) aka Queen Niche

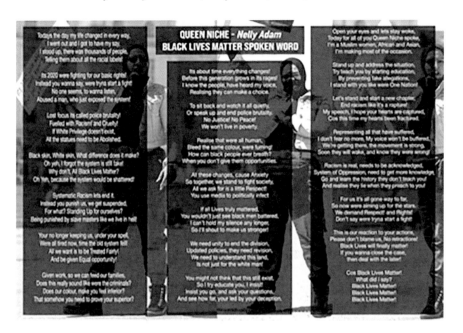

Today's the day my life changed in every way,
I went out and I got to have my say,
I stood up, there was thousands of people,
Telling them about all the racial labels!

It's 2020 were fighting for our basic rights!
Instead you wanna say, were tryna start a fight!
No one seems, to wanna listen,
Abused a man, who just exposed the system!

Lost focus it's called police brutality!
Fuelled with Racism! and Cruelty!
If White Privilege doesn't exist,
All the statues need to be Abolished.

Black skin, White skin, what difference does it make?
Oh yeh, I forgot the system is still fake!
Why don't, All Black Lives Matter?
Oh Yeh, because the system would be shattered!

Systematic Racism let's end it.
Instead you punish us, we get suspended,
For what? Standing Up for ourselves?
Being punished by slave masters like we live in hell!

You're no longer keeping us, under your spell,
We're all tired now, time the old system fell!
All we want is to be Treated Fairly!
And be given Equal opportunity!

Given work, so we can feed our families,
Does this really sound like were the criminals?
Does our colour, make you feel inferior?
That somehow you need to prove you're superior?

It's about time everything changes!
Before this generation grows in its rages!
I know the people, have heard my voice,
Realising they can make a choice.

To sit back and watch it all quietly,
Or speak up and end police brutality.
No Justice! No Peace!
We won't live in poverty.

Realise that we're all human,
Bleed the same colour, we're fuming!
How can black people ever breath?
When you don't give them opportunities.

Al these changes, cause Anxiety,
So together, we stand to fight society,
All we ask for is a little Respect!
You use media to politically infect!

If all lives truly mattered,
You wouldn't just see black men battered,
I can't hold my silence any longer,
So I'll shout to make us stronger!

We need unity to end the division,
Updated policies, they need revision,
We need to understand this land,
Is not, just for the white man!

You might not think that this still exist,
So I try educate you, I insist!
Insist you go, and ask your questions,
And see how far, you're led by your deception.

Open your eyes and let's stay woke,
Today for all of you Queen Niche spoke,
I'm a Muslim women, African and Asian,
I'm making most of the occasion.

Stand up and address the situation,
Try teach you by starting education,
By preventing fake allegations,
I stand with you like we're One Nation!

Let's stand and start a new chapter,
End racism like it's a rapture!
My speech, I hope your hearts are captured,
Cos this time my heart's been fractured.

Representing all that have suffered,
I don't fear no more, My voice won't be buffered,
We're getting there, the movement is strong,
Soon they will wake, and know they were Wrong!

Racism is real, needs to be acknowledged,
System of Oppression, need to get more knowledge,
Go and learn the history they don't teach you!
And realise they lie when they preach to you!

For us it's all gone way too far,
So now we're aiming up for the stars.
We demand Respect! and Rights!
Don't say were tryna start a fight!

This is our reaction to your actions,
Please don't blame us, No retractions!
Black Lives will finally matter
If you wanna close the case,
then deal with the latter

Cos Black Lives Matter!
What did I say?
Black Lives Matter!
Black Lives Matter!
Black Lives Matter!

Photograph courtesy of Simon O'Connor

A Room of One's Own: A Call for Inclusive, Sustainable Spaces to Empower, Protect & Support Women

CARDIFF

SISTERS OF SOLIDARITY

Claudia Boes makes a call for inclusive and sustainable spaces to empower, protect and support women.

This year marks the centenary of partial women's suffrage in the United Kingdom, when some women won the right to vote. 100 years on only 11 out of 40 Welsh MPs are women. In 2003, the National Assembly for Wales made waves as the first legislature to achieve 50:50 gender balance, however, has slipped back since then.

Research conducted by the House of Commons Library shows that between 2010 and now, 86% of the burden of austerity has fallen on women and this is set to rise considerably by 2020. According to the Women Budget Group, lone mothers representing 92% of lone parents are set to lose £8,790 per year and will experience an average drop in living standards of 18%.

The introduction of Universal Credit (UC) has a further detrimental effect on women and their families. Not only is UC changing the structure of families and increasing the dependency of some mothers on their male partner, as a rule a greater proportion of women's income is made up of benefits. For example, over fifty percent of housing benefit claimants in Wales are one-adult families and women. Even before taking the cost of childcare into consideration, the Child Poverty Action Group estimates that a single parent, working full time on the current 'national living wage' of £7.20 an hour, will have to work the equivalent of two extra months each year to make up for the loss of income due to the changes to the work allowance under UC.

After a decade of Westminster-led austerity, we desperately need spaces that build up, empower and protect women and communities. But existing organisations working with and providing essential services to women in Cardiff and Wales, are cut to the bone and are struggling to meet demand, not least Welsh Women's Aid, BAWSO and Women Connect First.

International Women's Day events this year linked in with the Global Women's Strike, a movement calling for solidarity between women—women of colour, indigenous, working class, disabled, migrant, Muslim, lesbian, queer and trans women. Women and their allies in Wales joined demonstrations in 50 countries who staged walkouts and/or met on the street. It was a public display of strength and resistance. If striking is the weapon of those who work, then the Global Women's Strike is a challenge to the assumption that women's labour, both in the workplace and in the home, should be underpaid, undervalued, or performed for free and with a smile. It goes back to the suffragettes who after decades of peaceful and reasonable campaigning by the suffragists adopted the motto 'Deeds Not Words'.

Wales has a long and proud tradition of Women's activism and campaigning, but 100 years after the suffragettes, women joining the Global Women Strike are equally exhausted from telling the same stories over and over again. Years of rapidly increasing insecurity and inequality, paired with rising living costs and sustained cuts to public services, have disproportionately affected women, BAME and working class women at that.

The Global Women's Strike is a call to and for action. Moreover, arguably mere survival is not enough for women, men, families and for Wales as a country. To put it in the words of one of the most prominent woman labour movement leaders, American socialist and feminist Rose Schneiderman 'the worker must have bread, but she must have roses, too'.

As part of its International Women's Day celebration, Cardiff hosted the 'A Room of One's Own' Pop-Up Women's Arts Centre located at Cathays Community Centre from 9th March to 11th March 2018. Organised by Cardiff Sisters of Solidarity, a Women's group campaigning against austerity and paid for through crowdfunding, 'A Room of One's Own' showcased the work of women and non-binary artists. The event presented a varied programme of music, banner-making, a book launch, dance, women's art and radical self-care workshops as well as food and opportunities for debate. Radical self-care refers to the idea that caring for yourself is not self-indulgence, but a necessity to keep going and looking after anyone else. For women, who often find themselves in the position of nurturers and carers, practicing self-love is essential.

Led by women but open to all individuals and community groups, it provided Cardiff's women's movement and activist scene with a temporary home and the opportunities to make connections, build alliances and take action on the many intersecting issues affecting women in Wales and worldwide. The response of both women offering to exhibit their work and running workshops as well as those attending was a true reflection of Cardiff's diversity and overwhelmingly positive.

Apart from celebrating International Women's Day in the year of the centenary of partial women's suffrage, the pop-up Women's Arts Centre also had wider strategic objectives. Together with the street celebrations on 8th March, the 'A Room of One's Own' Pop-up Women's Art Centre aimed to provide a space for Cardiff and surrounding areas' Women's Movement and Activist scene to meet, attend diverse events and build community. Despite the tremendous opportunities of social media to connect people, educate and raise awareness across the world, the recent #MeToo and #TimesUp campaigns being only two examples, online activism requires real-life follow-up to have a lasting impact.

A human need for tangible community and spaces that empower, protect and connect remains. This is particularly true for women. Women who are not only disproportionately affected by austerity as well as sexual and gender-based violence, but who are also socialised into and take on much of the caring for others. For Wales to be a country that works for and benefits everyone, we need more vibrant community-led spaces to celebrate, educate and empower people to make real connections. "A Room of One's Own" was an attempt to make activism accessible to a variety of groups including parents, carers and other groups underrepresented in the women's and activist movements through creating central, affordable, inclusive, and family friendly events. The success of the Pop-up Women's Centre and the overwhelming positive response from those who participated and attended, made a powerful case for long-term, accessible, and affordable community spaces.

The Women's Marches in January 2017, the #MeToo and #Timesup campaigns showing the epidemic proportion of sexual harassment and abuse and the growing support for the Global Women's Strike Movement are only the beginning. It's time for a change and for sustainable community development for the empowerment of Welsh women and communities to make real and lasting change.

First Published in *The Welsh Agenda*, 16th April 2018

Photograph courtesy of Taz Rahman

There's Room for Me Too

By Krystal S. Lowe

An open speech to the arts and cultural sectors, based on Krystal's lived experience as well as the lived experiences of artists who generously shared their lives with her.

I never want to be someone who spends more time discussing the things that need to change than I do actually changing them. There's Room for Me Too is about me doing my part to initiate change and to empower other people to make changes too. I wrote this text after gathering the experiences of other artists; while this text is written by myself it is an accumulation of many experiences. It is spoken for the young girls who are trying to decide who they are and what they want to be when they grow up; it's for the young women who are feeling they don't fit anywhere; and it's for those women who continually create and make in spite of the state of the world and sector.

To The Sector I love,

there's room for me too.

My intellect, my experiences, my thighs and my dark skin—

I'm not a threat to you.

My place is in every space where art is made and performed.

My creativity and my work will only improve the world.

There's room for me too.

So don't offer the lowest wage but showcase me on every poster

while simultaneously hiding me at the back of every stage.

At every age I have something to offer, something to give. I shouldn't have to prove

that my work is of worth simply because of differences you can't seem to see

past.

There's room for me too.

You hide behind words like 'classical'
as an excuse to continue racism, ableism, sexism, and exclusion.
You say there's no room in the writing for someone who looks like me,
as if excluding difference isn't centuries old;
an injustice created by the insecure that for some strange reason we refuse
to truly end.
Why have we allowed this system to continue to stand?
Tell the truth.
You prefer racism instead of change—don't you?

Hear me.
If your shows cannot showcase me—Write. New. Shows.

Don't call me lucky when I've earned all I have.
Don't write my name on applications for projects you never intended to hire
me for.
Don't tell me that my skin isn't an issue but the shape of my Black body is—
Black isn't just a colour, it's culture and frame,
and so much more even I'm still seeking to discover.
If you struggle to pronounce my name—
practice. Don't require
me to change it—once again—
to fit the aesthetic, you claim.

There's room for my identity too.

My identity isn't a trophy for you to hold above your head

so you can feel some sort of triumph

while I'm reduced to simply skin.

Simply skin.

There is more to me than simply skin.

Where do I begin?

I'm my mother's brown eyes,

And my father's high chin.

I'm the places I've been.

I'm the friends I've kept.

I'm the language I speak because it doesn't only belong to you.

Am nad ydyw'n perthyn i chi'n unig.

Mae lle i mi hefyd.

There's room for me.

Not 'women like me'—

part of a community or group as if I have no individual identity.

Look at me

and see

the fullness of the woman I am—

don't just label me B.A.M.E.

It's not enough to crowd your spaces with people who look like me,

while the high places are filled with people who look like you.

Where is the representation at the top of this pyramid?

No space?

Let's change the shape.

Make a place for difference in the board rooms and in the directors' chairs.

When there's representation where decision makers are

that's when change will truly start.

Do I look like 'another angry Black woman'?

Don't mistake my passion and unyielding fight against racism, ableism,

sexism, bigotry, exclusion,

and inaccessibility for something as simple as anger.

I have something far more powerful.

I have action. I have passion. I have fight. I have resolve.

You wish I was angry.

Then, you could dismiss me.

could pretend this is just a speech of abuse

instead, see, that this is me

shining a light on all that continues to go on in this sector that I love.

Silence doesn't equal peace.

Silence is loud and active.

If you're not actively a part of the solution than you're adding to the

problem.

The sector I see

isn't afraid of difference and change.

It's fuelled by diversity.

It seeks to engage all instead of the few

and values every person for their individual identity.

And I will not stop until the Sector I love, becomes all that it should be.

So, take down *your* barriers—

I'm well within reach.

There is room for me, and you.

Rachel Oliver, *Speak Up!*

Being Poor is not a Life Choice: Perspectives on Poverty & Class

By Rebecca Lowe

It is Boxing Day. We've polished off most of the leftover turkey with chips. Now we're onto cakes and Christmas pudding and, to be honest, I'm feeling rather bloated. My parents' 'upwardly mobile' friend is busy regaling us with the details of her latest cruise:

"Well, of course, it's my second time on the Mediterranean liners," she tells us. "The accommodation was ad-e-quate." (She stretches out the vowels to express her disappointment.)

"The French wine tour was good but, as you know, I'd visited Barcelona and Rome last year, so that part was a little dull. Lisbon was okay. Portugal was far too hot." I smile to myself at the way she can write off an entire country in a sentence.

After a while, sensing a lull in interest, the conversation moves to current affairs. Somebody mentions food banks. And it's now, right now when my defences are down, that she comes out with it. She wrinkles her face over a tray of vol-au-vents and says. "Well, these people on food banks. They're not *really* poor. They just can't handle their finances."

Well, that was a red rag to me. I'm not really an argumentative person. People who meet me for the first time often use words like 'quiet' and 'unassuming', though I seem to have become more outspoken as the years have gone by. My husband blames it on the people I mix with: "Those bloody socialist poets just make you angry!" I keep trying to explain to him that it isn't mixing with socialists that makes me angry, but it's the reality of living in a manifestly unjust capitalist dystopia run by Tory privileged idiots, that boils my blood. But he's having none of it.

"It's not the poor who can't handle their finances, but the rich!"

I hear my voice echo across the dinner table. Knives and forks are clattered onto plates. There's an expectant hush. I begin to wish I hadn't spoken, but I've started now, so I feel I have to go on.

"Whilst the rich have money sitting in investments making them more money, the entire system is stacked against those on lower incomes," I explain. "Hoarding money selfishly is morally much worse than having none.

And yet we venerate people who have lots of money and pour blame on those who don't. Why is that?"

At this point, I feel the need to backtrack a little...

I grew up with what I suppose you'd call a sharing economy. My Dad was a primary school teacher, my mum worked various part-time jobs, selling double glazing one week, or apple-picking the next. We covered bills but there wasn't loads left over. Every few months, as a family, we'd visit Nanny Dolly, and she'd lend us the floating fiver, (which I imagine with inflation would these days be the floating twenty-pound note). Nanny Dolly lived in a tiny house with a whirligig washing line I used to get told off for swinging on, and steep stairs leading to the two tiny rooms where she'd raised three children. Nanny Dolly was a collector of things and people and seemed to know everyone. When she was younger, she'd worked in the local corner shop, where she had a reputation for vaulting athletically over the counter whenever anyone needed assistance. If anyone had a baby and needed help, or someone close had died and they needed a shoulder to cry on, it was Nanny Dolly they called on. Whenever we visited, she'd have a selection of items lined up for us—bikes, school uniforms, toys, shoes, all passed on from others down the street whose children had outgrown them. And in return she'd pass on her things to others, including any presents we gave her. Nothing ever remained in her house for long. If she had few personal possessions left, it didn't seem to bother her; she was one of the most contented people I knew.

Growing up with this sort of philosophy, you can perhaps see why I find the idea of piling up excess wealth an alien concept. Most of the people I knew then, and most I know today, never had the option of making savings and investments. Beyond a small amount in the bank to cover emergencies such as the roof blowing off, (a very real concern when you live in a Welsh terrace at the top of a hill), almost everything goes on housing, food and basic living expenses.

There are entire sections of the media devoted to where best to stash your excess millions, but precious little on how to budget on a minimal and often unstable income—yet that's the reality for the majority of working people. The fact is, the poorer you are, the more expensive it is to live.

Take heating, for example. Most council tenants buy their energy via gas and electric meters, which are a notorious rip-off. People who can afford to set up direct debits are in a far stronger position and don't risk being cut off if they can't afford to put money in the meter. Meter cards must be topped up at the post office, meaning a cold and costly trip, often by bus, and impossible if you're a single parent, with kids in tow. Public transport in many parts of Wales is overpriced and unreliable, so this is another huge inequality.

Then there's the cost of food shopping. Those with a reliable, large pay cheque can afford to buy in bulk. But when you're eking your cash 'til the end of the month you tend to buy in smaller quantities which is vastly more expensive. The system is stacked against those who live in poverty and it's these hidden barriers which are not understood by those who live in relative comfort.

I'm back to thinking of Nanny Dolly again. Her husband (my Grandad) Bert, worked as an assembler in a pipe factory. When she was younger, before the kids came along, she took on a series of part-time jobs, one time working as a delivery driver (a job which ended spectacularly in her first week when she wrapped the horse and delivery cart around a lamppost) and another as a peeler in a pickled onion factory. As a teenager she'd joined her sisters, adding three years to her age to become a high-kicking dancer on Plymouth pier to make some holiday money. She was versatile, could spot an opportunity, and would give almost anything a try. But her aspirations and opportunities were limited by circumstance. My Dad's generation was the first to go to grammar school and then on to further education. It seemed to offer a way up, a path towards creating a more equal society. And yet, even for my generation, those inequalities were still *all* too evident. I remember, at university, one particularly pompous, privately-educated student telling me 'Well, of course, we're the cream of intelligence at this university', and me assuring him in no uncertain terms that I knew of children in my town's state school who were at least as intelligent as him but had just never been offered the same opportunities.

Nobody chooses to be poor. Nobody chooses to limit their opportunities or those of their children. The sad fact is that, over the past few years, wealth inequality has risen at an alarming rate. The UK, as a whole, has one of the worst levels of wealth inequality in Europe. In 2016 the richest ten per cent of households held 44% of all the wealth.

The coronavirus crisis has only served to highlight these divisions. Deaths in the most deprived areas have been more than double those in the least deprived. Viruses don't discriminate. Society does. Food poverty, cramped and overcrowded living conditions, money worries and job insecurity, plus the stress of working multiple jobs on minimal incomes—all of these add up to a less healthy lifestyle. Being poor is deadly.

I've lived at different ends of the income bracket. At best I was earning a decent wage as a copywriter in London. At worst I was claiming benefits, while struggling to pay off an overdraft which grew incrementally every day. I couldn't pay it. Banks discriminate against the poor. Being poor is unfeasibly expensive. Money keeps us afloat. It's easy, when you're wealthy, to praise the virtues of frugal living. But the reality is that being poor sucks. Having no money costs money. To the tune of fifty pence for every day you're overdrawn. But being rich makes you richer. Money in the bank generates money. For zero effort. Just a pat on the back from the bank for being rich. Nice work, if you can get it.

It was Basil of Caesarea, writing in the 4th Century AD, who came out with probably my favourite quote on wealth: "When someone steals another's clothes, we call them a thief. Should we not give the same name to one who could clothe the naked and does not? The bread in your cupboard belongs to the hungry; the coat unused in your closet belongs to the one who needs it; the shoes rotting in your closet belong to the one who has no shoes; the money which you hoard up belongs to the poor." And it was the son of a carpenter centuries before who said: "For what does it profit you to gain the whole world and lose your soul?"

Think about it for a moment. What is money actually *for*? For me, it's quite simple. Once you have enough—and by 'enough' I mean sufficient to pay for your basic needs and a little extra left over for emergencies and fun—the purpose of money is to help others. Because we live in a society. A society of people. Of course, some of our taxes are set aside for that purpose. That's the basic premise behind the Welfare State and the NHS, pillars of our society which, despite clapping for our doctors and nurses in public, our current government seems set on eroding and undermining.

But even after we've paid our taxes (and I've noticed the very wealthy are particularly good at avoiding that too), there is still no excuse for reaping vast profits whilst continuing to walk past others in desperate need. Not when you have more money than you can spend sitting in the bank, doing nothing but make you more money. Or sufficient to splash out on cruises that bore you because you've travelled round the world multiple times.

Does anyone honestly think that families would choose to subsist on food banks, if they didn't have to?

And here we sit, at Christmas, stuffing our faces with more food than we can possibly eat, celebrating the birth of a baby in a backstreet stable to an unmarried mother and carpenter father, who became penniless asylum seekers fleeing persecution from a tyrannical ruler. A baby who would grow up to say things like: 'It is easier for a camel to pass through the eye of a needle than for a rich person to enter heaven.' And you dare to tell me that the reason the poor are poor is because they can't handle money? It's a bit like telling the starving that the reason they are starving is because they can't handle bread. And I'm just not buying it. I'm not buying it at all.

Strangely enough, I've not been invited back for dinner this Christmas...

Rachel Oliver, *If I Only Had a Heart*

Entrapment

By MJ

In April 2020 we are already a few weeks into a national lock down—battling Covid-19, anxious and worrying for everybody. I am a single mum from Trethomas, in the Rhymney valley. I have two children, so I had a lot of anxieties about this whole situation. I also have two health conditions, physical and mental, so I was asked to shield for 23 weeks. Trying to keep both illnesses stable and take care of my children was challenging but I also loved having so much time with them. So I kept positive as much as I could and decided to get all the art stuff out and go into my own world with colours and music.

Then things got *really* dark for me as two people very close to my heart passed away. I was and still am devastated. I could not say goodbye. I also couldn't be with loved ones who were also grieving and devastated... people who needed me as much as I need them. I have never felt so lonely, useless, hopeless, angry, and hurt in my life, and had to keep all these emotions controlled as I was alone with my children. I kept reminding myself of how supportive everyone else had been... family, friends, neighbours. Me and my kids never went without anything, and I was and still am so grateful. This helped me see good in the world when I felt like I didn't want to be in it.

So, I went in the garden one morning and decided to switch off, not feel and stop over thinking.

I picked up my paint brush and used all the colours I had and got completely lost, just painting my mermaid who was trapped in a net, looking out at the world, and wanting to be with people who she loved and needed. Feeling angry at being trapped, sad, lonely. I realised I'd been painting my own feelings, and I love mermaids and colour, so this really helped the way I was feeling, made me smile, felt a bit more positive. Now every time I look at this piece I created; it reminds me that no matter how dark things get there are always bright colours to get you to a better place.

Osian Grifford, *The Rhondda Floods*

surround myself with busyness

by lloyd robson

y**ou** say i should cease sport & my attendance it brings my aggression to sore throat & dagger-eyed self-defeating extremities i will give myself a heart attack or cause some fuck to shit their pants which really is unnecessary considering the circumstances.

you say i should slow down with the booze it makes me think i'm seventeen years old not seventeen first time but seventeen & more so. cock of the walk up for a fight up for the eyeball psych out duel or a scrap i will lose while gaining the joyous experience of getting a bloody good battering & a black eye for the girls the women i could have if only i was single. the bottle over the back of the head from her husband when i'm not looking the prize of a cuckold the reward the excitement.

you say i should stop using drugs it confuses my attention intention & abilities to differentiate between real & imagined worlds they magnify & render invisible they split my already multi-divisible person fill life with irrelevant layers of reverberance & disturbance they shuffle my refusals.

you say i should exile extricate eradicate extradite disband debar & red card certain individuals from my mind even more than from my presence remove their cookie their worm their virus from my system but protectors have no update i battle with infection.

you say i should find peace with myself for myself & by myself & call a truce with the world & its people but trust & faith were tried & found treasonous in their claims deliberance deliverance & deliverers were conniving & brutal.

you say i should listen to myself & to what i once imagined. *pah!* i visualised goodness & wisdom, not shit shovels without heads nor handles & steaming piles of never vanishing issues. calm & simple pleasure not brainstorm & lightning bolt fusing the perceptions. midnight attacks, imaginings & interpersonal suicide bombers killers fiddlers queuing next to my bedside table.

you say i should compare what i want to what i have. i remind you i want to get through this better this & achieve such things if only i could have two minutes without questions. numb dumb & insensitive if only for an instant. who i wanted to be with who i didn't. i tell you i would like this but cannot remember past the concentrated insistence of the shadow i have become of him.

i remind you i live in a circle. you say i should square it. so i do all this.

i take you at your word & strip bare remove defining factors to see what remains of this shaft of flesh & the beacon & whistle that live in it. look deep down dark & light & honest into the prism the mirror the spotlite & i see the love the bitterness the brave dilemma the fear & still it leaves me

debilitated, not so vicious maybe, eaten by my history & its unhappiness reverberates even louder surer shaking my bones bruising the extremes of me loosening the appendages the eyes from their sockets the wax from my ears the juice from my sack the grease from my elbow the knock from my knees the nails from my toes & my fingers crease arthritically

& i can only decide not to listen to myself again for what i find is nothing without his influence. & what i want is me & me but what i find is me & him & i don't like my life like this.

i didn't see the betrayal coming from inside the wisdom. i didn't fathom the knife in the back would be knock on the door parcel in hand delivered by uniformed courier with a fucking great neon sign on his cap. i didn't realise i was knowingly signing cash on the dot for my own denial hoped i'd have the knowledge the suss the nous the reaction the wherewithal the half a fucking brain necessary to at least defend myself from my own experience dream & imagination.

& now that you have talked me into this now we chat friendly perched on the edge of things there is nowhere new for me to go but for plodding & plod i do not do so well. so *bbboing!* onwards i go bouncing rebounding ricocheting occasionally resting swirling swerving redirecting playing chicken blindfold kamikaze out of the sun veering exploding convincing myself that maybe through busyness comes solution directionless at warp speed maximum into space time & this limited down ticking existence & eventually one of these bumps will do for me unless i find the brake & pull in but then *aha!* the brake could well be the untimely shock to the system.

is it death? fuck death that's the least of my worries. death is a piece of piss take my word for it clips you or you choose to cease it's living or rather choosing how to with the greatest ease & success.

define success.

so i've seen my future. i know what awaits. but all you see is me sat here staring at myself & the blank page, going around in circles with the fleck in my eye my diaphragm stressed a head full of heritage & a deep breath braced desperately trying but not wanting to exhale nor face the next test

test what test? fuck that, it's experience.

first published in the collection *bbboing! & associated weirdness* by lloyd robson (Parthian, Wales, 2003, isbn 1 902638 29 8)

Rachel Oliver, *There's no Planet B*

Can blindness be desired: what have those eyes seen, to desire to see no more?

By Eric Ngalle Charles

Truly, when did your sun die? The light which once your eyes radiate. Your face darkened, your forehead has hornlike boulders is that the devil coming out? Uncle, yesterday she greeted you, like a black cat visiting a guillotine, you squirmed, that was Monday. You embraced her sister's son, with Judas's kiss. Dearest uncle when did you swallow death whole? When did you start the dance of an impostor? When did the Gods possess your spirit?

Dearest uncle, when did you start digging her mother's Grave? Yesterday she looked at the river which separates the villages. She sucked the back head of a black toad, its content glued under her tongue, to spit in your eyes, in blindness you would see. Maybe.

She could not breathe, the whole world had been deprived of air it seemed. As she sat on that stone, looking at her mother's kitchen. She could not find answers to any of the questions she was asking to herself.

Why her? She thought.

The intensity of this moment made her reach into her handbag. She brought out a scissors. She started cutting herself. First her ears, her nose, and finally she gouged out one of her eyes. She had simply had enough, she had asked the Gods many times to render her blind, they had ignored her request. With one eye, she looked at the ground, it was covered in red. Yet, the bleeding failed to carry her away from the darkness that had suddenly overtaken her.

Her uncle, why her?

The only thing that remained of her mothers' kitchen was the Iroko tree, Milicia excelsa, the great yielder of Timber as it is known by the people of the great plains of the south. A giant that grows to about 66ft above the ground with its pale dark and at times grey bark. Like her today, the Iroko tree bleeds and oozes milky latex every time it is damaged. She looked into the tree thinking how long it had been standing there? She remembered that line in

Chekhov's *'The Kiss'* "nights bring pensive thought".

She asked herself repeatedly the question that was taking her into these depths of despair. 'Can blindness be desired'?

She remembered the last story her mother told her a couple of nights ago before she returned into the forest to be with the ancestors.

Upon going to the market one Sunday morning, the millipede saw the stick insect on the side of the great Iroko three performing what looked like press-ups. Thinking the stick insect was sick, that maybe the stick insect was suffering from an advance form of Parkinson's disease, the millipede stopped to enquire.

'My friend, are you unwell?'

'Can I be of assistance to you?'

'What reasons have you got for suggesting I am sick?'

The stick answered folding its fists:

'As you can see, this tree has been here for four hundred years. It has been blocking the sun from reaching my crops. I am going to shake it until it falls to the ground. Please my friend, watch your mouth and stop disturbing me with all this your stupid question.'

'For the record, I am not sick. In fact, move run fast, move away from there. I can hear the Iroko shaking from its roots. It is about to fall. Run, let it not fall on you before the whole nation accuses me of killing you.'

While running away as fast as it could from the falling tree, the millipede came across the tortoise. Frightened, the tortoise who had never seen the millipede running that fast stopped and inquired as to the reason behind such haste. The millipede warned the tortoise of the impending danger. That the stick insect had gone mad and was going to uproot the Iroko tree and fell it to the ground. The tortoise laughed.

'The stick insect suffers from advanced Parkinson's'.

'Can't you see how it shakes.'

'Have you seen the size of the stick insect's hands.'

'Have you seen how skinny its legs are.'

'I bet you, the stick insect would die.'

'His generation would come and go.'

'The Iroko tree would still be standing.'

'My friend, pace yourself, pay no attention to what the stick insect is saying'.

'It has gone mad, I tell you.'

Six months later, on its way to the village market, the millipede came across the stick insect shaking on the same spot. Shocked to see the millipede, the stick insect shouted.

'Get out of the way. What if this tree falls on you?'

'What would the villagers say?'

'They would accuse me of witchcraft.'

'Remember what they did to late uncle Zingraf?'

'Get out of the way, please get out.'

'Is this not the same tree I saw you pushing six months ago?' Asked the millipede.

'Nothing has changed.'

'Stop this nonsense.'

As the stick insect continued its fight against the Iroko tree, the millipede looked up into the skies and shouted, pleading with the gods:

'Enu leya matoh.'

'Enu leya miroh.'

'Nazra weya weya weya ma Molikilikili ama.'

It begged the Gods to render it deaf and blind as it did not wish to see or hear the gibberish that was coming out of the mouth of the stick insect.

Sarah smiled, she lifted her eyes and looked at her mother's kitchen for the last time. She brought the scissors closer to her other eye.

Sarah Oneill, *Gammons*

Gammon in the Sky

By Gareth Twamley

A farm where some pigs fly and snowflakes are endangered. A farm where caring is sharing, and sharing is scaring. A farm dubbed *great* as it grates at good souls. A farm with soil so salty it makes Utah gravel seem sweet. A farm of thirty million pigs and a legendary status for plucky meat, quietly prospering below farmyard radar under the Suidae sky. Good animals creating and expressing, surviving the porcine oppression in the great sty. Domesticated herd, aghast at the greed of the biggest boars. Boss hogs fit to burst. Feeding frenzies for the few, not plenty for the many. Pig Pharma's on the cull, quietly dulling. Annulling good minds. Putrefying in chemical dip. Penned in intellects for profit. Favourite snouts spared the slaughter. Pot-bellied pigs in a palace. Lunching from a golden trough. Skinny runts look on, funding the feast with all they've got. Some eat each other, some just beaten. For others the only solution; saline, or smoke cos it's just a waste of time being woke. Good creatures can only do what they do, fighting through faeces and picking through swill. Avoiding vicious stamping hooves, living their best muddied lives. Choosing decency, choosing to fight without a fight. Drawing love, not blood in their sentient minds. Good creatures can only do what they do. Good creatures will continue to root.

The Battle of Trafalgar Square

By Tim Evans

Tim Evans, *Self Portrait*

A bottle sailed over my head, and I watched, amazed, as it shattered as if in slow motion, on a riot policeman's helmet. A group of crash-helmeted police turned and began to move rapidly towards us. I was holding my hands palms open down at my sides to make it crystal clear I was not throwing anything, and the man who had thrown the bottle had already vanished, but by now such niceties were irrelevant. A policeman ran straight at the guy beside me and struck him a nasty blow on the head. He fell sideways into the arms of his friend and they staggered away. I realised that actually arresting us was the last thing on their minds. I leaped over the fallen crash barrier lying on the theatre steps and ran as fast as I could up towards Trafalgar Square, heart thumping.

It had been different twenty minutes ago. The police—not riot police, but ordinary Metropolitan coppers—had been trying to cram the demonstrators into Trafalgar Square. But they had completely underestimated the size of the 200,000-strong march. Peaceful protestors were being pushed and squeezed into an area far too small to hold them. We started chanting 'Hillsborough! Hillsborough!"—for it was only a year ago that ninety-six Liverpool supporters had been killed in Hillsborough stadium as police attempted the exact same tactics. But the police kept pushing. The crowd started pushing back, more and more joining in. Then with a roar from the crowd the police lines broke. Panic. They turned and ran. I was astounded. It was the first time I had seen police run away from protesters, rather than the other way around. A roar of triumph went up as they escaped down Whitehall. Traffic cones and empty cans flew after them. A fat little inspector was running as fast as his legs could carry him, hand clamped on his peaked cap and naked fear in his eyes. It was like something out of an old Keystone Cops movie. As they ran down Whitehall towards Parliament Square, hundreds of demonstrators chased after them, exhilarated and triumphant after being penned in for over an hour and now free to pursue their tormentors. They chased them down Whitehall and then milled around, smiling and laughing. No-one could quite believe what had happened. Chants of "No poll tax!" echoed off the nearby theatres, offices and pubs. Outside some of the pubs a few drinkers smiled and gave thumbs up signs. Others, pints in hand, joined in the chant.

Everybody, apart from the rich, and most, but not all, of the Tory party, hated the poll tax. To make a student nurse in a pokey little flat pay the same level of domestic rates as a billionaire in their country mansion was so obviously unjust that tens of thousands of people up and down the land had already joined in the protests and mini-riots that had broken out in the most unlikely of places: little leafy villages in the south-east of England, towns with Tory MPs in the commuter belt around London, picturesque seaside towns in Devon and Dorset. The Trafalgar Square riot was unexpected and entirely spontaneous. I certainly didn't expect it, and I didn't expect what followed either.

Thatcher and the Tories had spent the 1980s smashing the unions. The biggest defeat, obviously, was that of the miners in 1984-85, followed by the vile Murdoch's lockout of the printers in 1986 at Wapping. The National Union of Mineworkers was the most highly politicised union in Britain, and the

Tories had never forgotten the way they had toppled the Heath government in 1974. The print unions operated the most cast-iron closed shop in the country. These unions had real power and could not be permitted to continue by a right-wing Tory government intent on opening the way to the neoliberal economy we now suffer under so grievously. So the idea was to provoke strikes and smash them.

By 1989 the Thatcher government was riding high. People may be familiar with the Greek term 'hubris'—excessive arrogance which leads to a massive comeuppance. "Pride comes before a fall" is another way of putting it. The poll tax was just such a step too far. The Tories' plan to eviscerate the unions involved what were called 'salami tactics.' You know how a stick of salami is sliced up into thin slices? Well the idea was to take on one union at a time—one slice at a time. Given the narrow-minded sectionalism of much of the British union movement at this time this wasn't too difficult. If one union's members looked like taking action in solidarity with those in struggle, the Thatcher government, in collusion with employers, threw them some crumbs to pacify them. Then they would get on with the serious business of defeating whichever union they had in their sights. By 1989 the Tories reckoned they had weakened both the unions and local left-wing councils sufficiently to impose the jewel in Thatcher's crown, the poll tax. It was first introduced in Scotland, where people rarely voted Tory anyway, and was due for implementation in April 1990 in England and Wales. Salami tactics couldn't really be applied with the poll tax—it affected everyone. And that was where, for Thatcher, things began to fall apart. A week before its implementation, on 31 March, the demo came about.

The Labour Party leadership, under Neil Kinnock, did not support a campaign of non-payment, neither did it play any serious part in the resistance. Their official line was to pay up and vote Labour in the next election, whenever that was. But many families, especially large families of low-paid workers crammed into one house, faced a massive increase in bills and simply couldn't afford to pay. Waiting for a Labour government was not a feasible option. However, tens of thousands of Labour voters, and thousands of brilliant rank-and-file Labour activists ignored their leaders, and joined the campaign. The slogan was 'Can't Pay—Won't Pay.'

After the police had been chased out of Trafalgar Square, they brought in the riot squads. Crash-helmeted and with round shields and truncheons, they emerged, like something out of *Star Wars*, from the neighbouring side streets and moved up Whitehall towards us. Mounted police, also crash-helmeted, followed behind. Not wishing to give ground, many of us moved off the road and onto the steps of the various theatres that lined Whitehall, waiting to see what happened next. Bottles and cans were lobbed, and as it became clear that the snatch squads were less interested in making arrests than in giving us a good battering, we fled too. By now, I was separated from the St Albans contingent with whom I'd travelled down by coach. I looked around but could see no familiar faces.

By the time I reached Trafalgar Square again it was empty of police. They had all disappeared, apart from the riot squads and cavalry that were coming up Whitehall. Many protesters turned to face them. Cones, cans and placard sticks flew through the air, but still the snatch squads kept on coming. Hundreds of us milled around the fountains and at the foot of Nelson's column. By now, protestors had set fire to the hoardings and scaffolding surrounding an office development close to the South African embassy. Flames and smoke licked into the sky and drifted across Trafalgar Square. Suddenly I became aware of more police, mounted now, coming at speed down the road from St Martin's in the Fields. A young woman went down under the horses' hooves as the cavalry division galloped in the direction of Whitehall. With incredible good luck she seemed unhurt, if a bit dazed, and scrambled to her feet as her friends dragged her away. A roar of anger came from the crowd, and missiles came flying through the air as the mounted police continued to career past in what seemed a provocative and pointless exercise.

What was so notable on 31 March was the anger and the willingness by protestors to face up to the police. In part this was due to the latter's inept and arrogant attitude. The Met had spent much of the 1980s attacking strikers and pickets, with Thatcher's full backing. Two miners died on picket lines in 1984, and in 1986 a young man was killed by a TNT lorry sweeping out of Murdoch's Wapping plant. Nobody ever faced any charges. The Met were often drafted into pit villages, since the authorities often feared to use local police, whose friends and family might well be on strike. And the Met went in hard and nasty and used provocative tactics, waving twenty pound notes at picketing miners as they swept past them in coaches, escorting scabs into the colliery. At the same time the BBC manipulated the news to edit out any police violence, while amplifying any violent reactions by the miners. So, by 1990, the Met felt they could deal with any resistance by simply battering people off the streets. On 31 March they found out how wrong they were.

The riot was not just the result of misjudged police tactics, however. We had had over a decade of Thatcher. That had meant not just attacks on the trade unions and left-wing councils, not just the abolition of the Greater London Council and the Inner London Education Authority, not just the Falklands War and calls from some Tories to hang Nelson Mandela, not just Section 28 and the driving out of any discussion of homosexuality from the school curriculum, not just the persecution of New Age Travellers and rave culture, but, crucially, wholesale privatisation through the selling off of previously state-owned industries to the Tories' cronies in the City. By 1989-90 the British working class had been given a sustained kicking for a long time. Anger levels were very high. The poll tax uprising was like a lightning conductor for years of pent-up frustration and fury that on 31 March exploded onto the streets.

As the portacabins and scaffolding blazed, and as protestors battled it out with riot police in Trafalgar Square, crowds surged round the side of the South African Embassy. A chair was hurled, and a side window was smashed in. Flames suddenly licked up the side of the building. Another roar went up from the crowd, then wild cheering. The embassy was a symbol of apartheid. The 1980s had seen massive and courageous battles by the black South African working class, as new trade unions there had taken on the government and the townships had exploded in anger. We watched, astonished, as part of the building took fire. For a few brief minutes we thought we were witnessing the burning down of the embassy. It didn't happen. Somebody inside the building was turning the full force of several fire extinguishers on the flames. I learned that in a news bulletin later in the day scenes from the South African township of Soweto were shown. People were dancing in the streets with placards reading 'No Poll Tax'. There was, of course, no poll tax in South Africa, but by now the attempted burning of the embassy was world news. International solidarity is more powerful than we think.

Wild skirmishing and full-scale fighting continued in Trafalgar Square for several hours. Eventually the police managed to push many protestors out of the square and into the West End. Why they did this, rather than south, towards the Thames, was unclear, but it was a major mistake. It was now that posh shop and restaurant windows got smashed, expensive car showrooms were attacked, BMWs were overturned and set on fire, and protestors continued hand-to-hand fighting with the police, who usually seemed to be getting the worst of it. As night fell, there was also widespread looting. Many who were not on the original demonstration joined in the general chaos. The most serious rioting in a century gripped central London.

By this time, I was trying again to find the St Albans contingent, without success. There had been several elderly and disabled people on our coaches, and it turned out that my best friend John Wangford, a hospital porter and one of the kindest people you could hope to know, had spent most of the afternoon looking after a few of them and had seen none of the chaos I had witnessed. The coaches were lined up on the Embankment, but in what seemed like a purely punitive measure, lines of police had heavily cordoned off the area, making it impossible to access. By now I was exhausted and hungry, and after a huge detour down to one of the other bridges and a couple of tube journeys across an underground system crammed with demonstrators, I managed to get to Kings Cross and took a train back to St Albans. I was lucky, as St Albans was a relatively short journey away. How people from Wales and the North of England managed to get home that night god only knows.

The poll tax riot marked not just the end of the poll tax, but the end of Thatcher. Tory grandees watched the news bulletins in horror as upturned Alfa Romeos burned on the streets of the West End, and police fled from angry mobs. Although the tide was already turning, she went from being 'the Iron Lady' to 'a bloody liability' on that single afternoon in March. The men in suits from the 1922 Committee and, indeed, members of her own Cabinet, came visiting, some of them threatening to resign if she stayed. She finally resigned on 28 November 1990, leaving Downing Street in tears, to the delight of the miners, steelworkers, printers, and others she had cast on the scrap heap.

Personally, I'd have preferred to have seen her driven out by a general strike rather than a riot, but, hey, a result's a result and I wasn't complaining.

The photograph itself is from the Welsh Industrial and Maritime Museum's Collection and is a photo labelled *'Working the Rolls at Tredegar Ironworks in 1912.287'*, published in the book *Welsh Steel* by Robert Protheroe-Jones. Drawing adapted by Tim Evans.

Narky Little Poltergeist

By Gareth Twamley

Fionn Wilson, *Southgate Bus Station* (2019)

He alighted the darkened doorway, his chosen exit. While he couldn't see his shadow in the corridor, it was there lurking with dastardly intent. He could feel it poking him. He heard it laughing at him and ribbing him like a narky little poltergeist.

He felt his way along this murky channel, braving the strain of this torrid stroll with his dark self, unsure of where he was going... Or why he was going there.

Suddenly, his pace quickened a factor of three. A sense of urgency drove him through the darkness. Rapid! Squelches became splashes. A march to a gallop. Careering headlong into pure pitch black. Hands and wrists grazing brutalist walls as he went. Bare knuckles bleeding. Agitated blood trailing in his wake.

Suddenly... Unexpectedly, he was there. The place he'd hoped to find. Shadow nowhere to be seen, felt nor heard. Pure stillness. Unadulterated silence.

He'd sought this moment. He'd reached the void. The nothing that is everything. The light that is the dark. The singularity of solitude. He stood, motionless. His pulsing heart suddenly shattered.

It was clear. This was it. There was no more. He sobbed inconsolably into the emptiness and wished to go home. He hadn't realised, but he was home.

Wilf

By J. Brookes

Photograph of graffiti art courtesy of Dave Lewis

Wilf was getting out. It was being tapped on the pipes all night: tappity tappity tap...

Wilf is getting out...

Every year for 30 years an appeal had been lodged on his behalf, and every year the most important judges on the most important benches on the most important circuits had laughed: 'Wilf? Fat chance...', and back the lawyers would go to their chambers to prepare next year's assault. And now, at last, success!

No-one could imagine HMP Grimlands without Wilf, he was a legend: 'It won't be the same old place...' prisoners told each other. Some tears were shed. Even the staff were excited.

'Rumbold,' said the governor to his deputy on the morning of Wilf's release, 'will you bring me Wilf's file?'

Rumbold went to the filing cabinet and came back with a shabby folder which he laid on the governor's desk. The governor opened it. What it contained was a poem called 'Mum' and a picture of a watermill, both the fruits of a brief art therapy and creative writing course that an idealistic warder called Dibden had tried to establish in the early 80s. 'Mum' went like this:

> *You bore me like a sack of coal,*
> *You raised me like a loaf of bread,*
> *You loved me like a sausage-roll,*
> *And now, old Mum, you're dead.*

'Hmmm,' said the governor, 'not exactly Alfred Lord Byron.'

'No indeed,' said Rumbold. Might be code of course.'

'Must be,' said the governor, and raised the picture of a watermill, which, on closer inspection, might have been a camel, and placed it on the radiator.

'Well, what are you waiting for, Rumbold, fetch him, fetch him...'

Down the clanking staircase Rumbold went, along the clanking corridors, and into the clanking dining-hall where breakfast was underway. A large banner made of stolen prison sheets was suspended above the tea-urns. GOOD LUCK WILF it read in large, black boot-polish letters. 'Anyone seen Wilf?' asked Rumbold above the din of chewed fried bread. At the name 'Wilf' some of the braver fellows essayed a round of 'For He's a jolly Good Fellow', though no-one could say exactly where Wilf was.

'He must be in his cell packing' said one of the officers, so Rumbold clanked through the jubilant breakfasters and down to the cellblock.

'Wilf? Cell number....' said the duty officer considering his list '...one or other of them anyway...', so one by one the cells were unlocked, the inmates paraded, and their names enquired. None were Wilf.

There had been some hangings that morning, so Rumbold headed out to the execution area in case Wilf had been accidently done away with. The corpses were still strung-up, turning slowly in the light morning breeze.

'No Sir,' said the hangman, who was folding his mask, 'a Gubbins and a McPhee, I believe.'

By mid-morning Rumbold had visited the workshops, the library, the laundry room and the gym. He's had the punishment block turned-out, the Visitors' Centre turned upside-down and the chapel turned inside-out. He'd been over to the women's block and had a pickpocket called Mrs Wilfson lightly tortured. He'd been onto the roof where a couple of disgruntled lifers were spinning tiles down at the riot-squad mustered below. He'd even been through the officers' rest room, ticking his men off one by one as they chalked their cues and raised their tankards.

Everybody knew Wilf, had seen him, when was it? recently anyway. 'Ask Bert or Alf or Nobbie' he was told, and Bert or Alf or Nobbie remembered seeing Wilf, well, not long ago, and why didn't he ask Len or George or Doug?

Back Rumbold went through the clanking corridors and up the clanking stairs to where the governor was waiting.

*

That afternoon thirty years of CCTV was run through, and though two men who *might* have been Wilf were spotted, one brushing his teeth in 1987 and one playing ping-pong in 1991, after a little enquiry these turned out to be Ledgewidge and Dodgson.

Part of the problem was that no-one could, with any exactitude, remember what Wilf looked like. Most people were confident of certain details: Warder Thompson recalled a big nose, Warder Wilkins remembered handlebar moustaches, Rumbold brought to mind a wooden leg, and the governor himself a glass eye. It was perplexing. And the perplexity only increased when a musing Rumbold turned the 'Mum' poem over and read P. Crutchly on the back, a signature that corresponded to 'Wilf' no more than the C. Finchly that the governor discerned in brown paint on the back of the picture of a camel or watermill.

*

That evening Wilf's release was headline news. Paper sellers cried out for extra bales, several bonfires were lit, and there were cheery knees-ups in certain sorts of pubs up and down the land till well after midnight.

Fighting for Justice: The Story of the Cardiff 3

By Des Mannay

In 1990 Yusef Abdullahi, Stephen Miller and Tony Parris were wrongfully convicted of the murder of Lynette White. Here Des Mannay recalls the campaign to clear their name.

It was Wednesday 13th of April 2005, when I got a telephone call. "Have you seen the front page of today's echo?" I walked up to a vendor, picked up a copy and could hardly believe my eyes. 'Lynnette Murder: Ex-Cops Arrested. Five Retired Police Face 'Lies' Quiz' the headline screamed. Staring out was the face of Lynette White. It pitched me back to another newspaper and another headline.

Now it's 1990, and I'm on my way to a newsagent where I pick up a copy of *Caribbean Times*. The collapse of communism in Eastern Europe, Poll Tax and the first Gulf War featuring George Bush senior are all headline news. I head for a 'shared house' occupied by a number Socialist Workers Party members: Caroline, Dave and Sophie. We start making placards for the evenings Anti War vigil amid cups of tea and conversation. Then the headline on the newspaper hit me 'Who Killed Lynette? Cardiff: Three Gaoled For Life'. It stated: 'Cardiff's black community has expressed bewilderment at the British press's lack of interest in the longest running murder case in British legal history. The case of the horrific 1988 murder of Lynette White seems to have concluded with three men receiving life sentences. However, the local community continues to pose questions which very few people are willing to answer.'

It went on to point out that the police were originally looking for a white man covered in blood, that the five defendants were black and that forensic tests showed none of the men's blood types matched samples found at the crime scene. The article also quoted locals hopeful of campaigning to free those imprisoned: "There is something sour smelling about this case and it would seem they wish to buy our silence by giving us two of the boys while they hold onto the rest, that will not wash the stench away." As this began to sink in Sophie asked: "Do you think this could turn into something like the

Guildford Four or Birmingham Six ... the Cardiff Three?"

From here, images flood into my mind of the three faces emblazoned on a banner of Yusef Abdullahi, Stephen Miller and Tony Parris, robbed of their freedom, and Lynette White robbed of her life; her name synonymous now with the words 'Cardiff Prostitute'. But she had a past; short-lived though it was. Born in 1968, into a household of frequent rows, she was looked after by her grandmother from 18 months until she was four. After her father was released from prison and settled down with another partner, Lynette returned to live with them, though she would often spend weekends with her 'nanna'. This continued until she was 12 and her grandmother committed suicide. Lynette was devastated. She drifted through school, leaving without qualifications at 16. The affection she had for her nanna was transferred to her aunt Lyn, who recalled: "Lynette had lovely skin and a fantastic personality. I used to call her my protégé. We'd say she would be a model and look after me in my old age. That was the dream we used to giggle over". That dream never came true. At 17 she had drifted into prostitution. At this time she was living with her first boyfriend Mark. A year later she met Stephen Miller. She worked as a prostitute up until St Valentine's day 1988 when she was stabbed more than 50 times, her left breast almost severed and her throat cut through to the spine. This tragedy led to legal farce, which is where the Cardiff Three story begins.

Initially the police were searching for a white man covered in blood—an artist's impression appeared on the police's murder poster along with a photo of Lynette. Yet nine months later the police arrested five black men of whom three were imprisoned for Killing. None of 150 fingerprints and blood samples at the scene of the crime matched any of the accused, and all three had alibis. Their conviction essentially rested upon one thing: the partial confession of Lynette's last boyfriend, Stephen Miller, who had a mental age of 11 and confessed after six days, on his 19th interview, in circumstances which Forensic Psychologist Dr. David Shepherd later described as "oppressive", and in breach of the Police and Criminal Evidence Act. It also rested on a bedrock of racism.

The trial of Cardiff 3 took place not in Cardiff but Swansea, with the Docks area of Cardiff, where the three hailed from, described as "a nocturnal world, an upside-down world where people carry knives". It was statements such as this which led to a feeling that the multi-cultural Butetown community was on trial. But this portrayal of the Docks population as an underclass, however, is symptomatic of Tiger Bay folklore imposed from outside. In *Bloody Valentine—A Killing In Cardiff* this is revelled in by John Williams who declares: "Alex knows what it's like, as do many of the Butetown women, when the only work open to their men folk tends to be outside the law." Whereas Peter Alexander, on the other hand, has a more pragmatic outlook: "The problem for black people becomes circular, being unemployed or having a rotten poorly paid job makes it difficult to get housing. Living in a run-down area makes it less likely that children will obtain the more stimulating education that middle class school students can expect. Lack of qualifications makes it more difficult to get a decent job. Involvement in crime then becomes more likely; so too does mental illness. Both further reinforce the problems of finding employment ... this reality helps to maintain a popular image 'the average black' which fits closely to the racist stereotype."

Racism, Resistance and Revolution

At the trial it was this stereotype which was found guilty. Whether the boys in the dock, or the Docks boys themselves fitted this image was irrelevant. (As a matter of fact, despite job losses in coal, steel and docks industries, at that time unemployment in Butetown had fallen by 3.7% while it was rising in South Glamorgan as a whole).

There was one more thing that had a less obvious impact on the fate of the Cardiff 3—the redevelopment of the Docks area itself. This had begun in 1984, reaching a climax with the activities of the Cardiff Bay Development Corporation in the late 1980's. As Rob Imrie noted on the fledgling development of the Bute East Dock: "What is particularly worrying... is the presumption against 'low order' uses like local industry, in favour of more marketable, or profitable, land uses, such as up market housing, offices and recreation."

Many of those involved in the Cardiff Three Campaign believed that the police were under pressure to solve the case because of the redevelopment —having an unsolved murder nine months on was bad for business. Former Councillor Betty Campbell claimed that Butetown will cease to exist, and as Huw Thomas points out, racism became a key factor in how the local population was "disinherited." The Cardiff Bay Business Forum is coyly discreet about this: "Many parts of the Bay... lie close to socially disadvantaged residential areas which... cannot provide sufficient numbers of people with the kind of skills needed by Bay businesses. This means that staff have to be recruited from outside the south of Cardiff." Malik Abdullahi put it another way: "We've always been ignored, but now if you want to move, you get a council house outside of this area straight away. They want to get us as far away as possible from the Docks now."

The Cardiff Three campaign started in earnest from February 1991, after a meeting of 300 people in Butetown. At this early stage, Channel 4's Black Bag made programmes about the case, but to have any chance of success, the campaign had to get its message heard loud and clear outside of the community. After much debate it was decided to make a concerted effort to seek affiliations with trade unions and other bodies. Some voiced worries that these people "weren't concerned with the suffering of a few black families". These fears were dispelled at a memorable AGM of Cardiff NALGO (now UNISON), which the campaign was invited to address. As campaign member Julian Goss remembers it: "A delegation addressed the meeting, and was asked to wait outside whilst a lively debate took place. Resourceful as ever, we found a way to eavesdrop... Nothing could be more educational than seeing black and white workers arguing for the right to affiliate with the campaign." The debate centred on whether this was a 'trade union issue' or not. This was dealt with by NALGO member Ted Adey: "Unions don't merely represent the people. Unions are the people. Most people, individually, have little power. Unions are, in a way, ordinary people trying to claim for themselves some influence over decisions that shape all our lives. Through trade unions, pressure can be brought on governments over a whole range of issues that affect us but also, no less important, we can fight for fair and equal treatment for the individual regardless of race, sex or religious beliefs and support policies that highlight and fight injustice."

The branch affiliated with the campaign. And so did the union nationally.

From then on, affiliations flew in from branches of CPSA, EQUITY, MSF, NALGO, NAPO, NUJ, NUPE and other unions, and Trades Councils, strengthening a campaign which already had the support of campaigning organisations such as Liberty, and anti-racist groups. I was a student at the time but became totally immersed in the campaign. When it came to it I sacrificed my course. Because of my socialist politics I looked after the trade union side of things, in which I was greatly assisted by a number of activists associated with Socialist Worker.

The backbone of the campaign, however, came from the Abdullahi and Parris families. Malik and Alex turned their house—kids and all—into the campaign headquarters. Malik had become obsessed with exposing every lie uttered in the trial and had no doubt about the innocence of the three. When I went round to volunteer my services—equally sure of their innocence—Malik kept me there for three hours, only letting me go after he'd given me several files of more evidence to read and return. The Parris family were dignified throughout the whole campaign, in the kind of way you imagine US Civil Rights activists like Rosa Parkes had been. They all had to endure the fact that their father died whilst Tony was still in prison and the image of him in handcuffs at the funeral won't go away. His brother Lloyd was like a rock throughout and as the campaign grew, so did these families in stature.

The campaign organised a number of public meetings and speaking tours, and we even organised two well-attended demonstrations, one of which included Civil Rights activist Rev. Al Sharpton. By this stage we were occupying the moral high ground, but as John Davies, Lord Gifford and Tony Richards point out: "When a community begins to assert its own dignity and to organise towards that end... it is likely to become the target of particular police attention and harassment." This was certainly true in Malik's case. His house was raided three times, and he was held for questioning, and finally charged with affray, violent disorder and carrying an offensive weapon. He was acquitted.

The boys were finally released on appeal December 1992. As Lloyd Parris recalls: "I can remember when the Cardiff Three were released. It was a bittersweet moment. Everyone was in the Paddle Steamer pub, drinking and being happy, but I couldn't get into that. All I could think was that they shouldn't have been inside in the first place, and how my whole family, especially my mum, had suffered."

Thirteen serving and former police officers were eventually charged with conspiring to put the Cardiff Three away. The police corruption trial collapsed in December 2011. It had been claimed that another set of documents that should have been disclosed to the defence had been shredded. The documents were later discovered in South Wales Police headquarters.

This is an updated version of an article originally published in issue 175 of *Planet*.

Bibliography

Alexander, Peter. *Racism, Resistance and Revolution*, Bookmarks, 1987.
Borrill, Rachel. 'Who Really Killed Lynette White?' *Independent* 22/11/1991.
Davies/Gifford/Richards. 'Political Policing in Wales', *WCCPL*, 1984.
Elderton, Jane. 'Police Made us Scapegoats', *Socialist Worker*, 1/ 2/ 1992.
Forum News, November 1992 'Trading Spaces.'
Hammond/Young. 'Lynette Murder: Ex-cops arrested', *South Wales Echo* 13/4/2005.
Imrie, Rob. 'Shape up or Ship Out: the Redevelopment of Cardiff Docks', *Radical Wales*, Spring 1989.
Kimber, Charlie. 'Former Cardiff Cops Arrested', *Socialist Worker* 23/4/2005.
Mannay, Des. 'A Tale of Racism Rage and Injustice', *Socialist Worker* 13/5/1995.
Massive, Mikey. 'Who Killed Lynette? Cardiff: Three Gaoled for Life', *Caribbean Times* 11/12/1990.
1991 Census, 'Profiles 1971-91 South Glamorgan County Council Electoral Divisions.'
Socialist Worker 3/10/1992, 'Cardiff 3 Man up in Court.'
South Glamorgan County Council, 'South Glamorgan's Unemployed: Distribution and Characteristics', October 1990.
Thomas, Huw. 'Europe's Most Exciting Waterfront', *Planet*, October/November 2000.
Toolis, Kevin. 'The Game of Love and Death', *Weekend Guardian*, 11-12/5/1991.
Union City News, December 1991 'Not a Union Issue?'
Williams, John. *Bloody Valentine—a Killing in Cardiff*, Harper Collins 1995.

Photograph courtesy of Taz Rahman

The Decisive Moment: Documenting Activism in the Digital Era of Citizen Journalism

By Taz Rahman

Cardiff-based professional photographer, Taz Rahman cut his teeth as a 'people' photographer on the streets of Cardiff between the 2015 General Election and the Sister March (CSOS) against Donald Trump's inauguration in January 2018. His work boasts at least 70 assignments, having photographed almost every protest organised in Cardiff since. He's covered the anti-austerity, feminist and transgender rights demonstrations, environmental barricades, anarchist gatherings, redundancy protests, Israel-Palestine activism, and large rallies against local arts funding cuts. His work has made it to the front pages of national tabloids, as well as the politics pages of The Guardian *and* HuffPost *in the UK, and even as far as China, USA, India, and Israel. He is the founder of 'Just Another Poet,' Wales' first Youtube poetry channel and was awarded a bursary and writing commission by* Literature Wales *in 2020. He has been editing the legal news blog LawNewsIndex.com since 2011.*

I am a poet and photographer who has always been fascinated by stories of protest, in particular: the depiction of protestations by literary and more literal observers. During my time as a freelance photojournalist, I have relished being at the forefront of protest rallies with my back to the world. I've never quite experienced adrenaline like it; walking backwards, trying to keep up, snapping at the heels of passionate activists.

'Gerontion' by T. S. Eliot, explores the inner thoughts of an old man who hadn't fought in the war, but he alludes to WWI which ravaged Europe in the early 1900s. Unlike Eliot's *The Waste Land*, which deals with the effect of war as a backdrop, there is no direct reference to the participants of war in this poem. Philosophically, Eliot was sympathetic to Eastern religious traditions of Buddhism and aspects of Hinduism, both of which see life in more cyclical terms of continual death and rebirth until nirvana—rather than the monotheistic tradition, spanning from Judaism to Christianity and later, in Islam, whereby creation is followed by death, purgatory and the notion of a final resting place of eternal hell or heaven. I believe that there is something of the 'cyclical' in the process of protesting, in the sense that they never *really* end, and the struggle is continual; with the same friendly faces showing up at each protest, regardless of the cause.

Since I was old enough to read the news, and from my first memory of witnessing political activism in the UK during the Poll Tax demonstrations (which notably ended the long political career of Margaret Thatcher), I wanted to make sense of what was being reported. During this time, protests in certain sections of the Islamic community were brewing; with some Muslims opposed to the publication of Salman Rushdie's *The Satanic Verses*. I watched the fall of Berlin Wall on TV, learned words such as: 'communist,' 'fascist' and 'fanatic' on the pages of the *Sunday Times* and the *Sunday Mirror*. I couldn't help noticing that the undertone of almost all political reporting was this narrative surrounding a battle between good and evil. I then started to question the nature of good and evil, but such questions wouldn't really gain a defined traction in my thought-process for a few more years, until I came to university in Cardiff to study philosophy. The studies did not amount to finding any solutions, but instead, resulted in a deeper appreciation of the nature of 'struggle' itself and a profound opposition to any absolutist belief. Thursday afternoon lectures on German Idealism, spearheaded by Hegel's 'dialectic,' which in simple terms refers to the interplay of opposing historical forces, left me with the distinct conclusion that humanity's struggle for rights is perpetual and a continual process through all ages, so protestation is almost a condition of human existence.

Surprisingly, as a photojournalist, I'm not great in crowds and in those early days of documenting protests, I truly struggled to negotiate my way through the mass of people, whilst trying to understand the technical challenges of finding the best position for a unique perspective. This changed after the third rally I had attended: some of the photos I had been submitting to photographic agencies such as *Demotix* and *Alamy Live News*, had been accepted, including the ones I took at the Transgender Rights protest against the Cardiff University annual lecture delivered by Germaine Greer, and continue to be published to this day. Beyond the national and international publications, my photos have been circulated within social media networks to raise awareness of issues, which probably serves as my own small contribution to any of the movements I witnessed.

For most of my protest photography career, I have watched the world through a ten-year-old second-hand Canon 5D and a Sigma 50mm EX DG f1.4 lens, often with a plastic carrier bag wrapped around my magnesium-alloy "cutlass," in case the Welsh rain penetrated the camera's weather seals. I was there in T. S. Eliot's 'warm rain' as a mere observer, not as a banner-waving activist. My politics have always been to the left of centre, but with great sympathy for the individual's right to exercise their minds and logically form a political opinion. I sympathised with the core objectives of the causes I photographed, but sometimes, I felt compelled to be there because the national press, and even the local media, mostly ignored small-scale local activism. My presence was less about political activism, but more a sense of loyalty to the local story and what I viewed as the roots of an unequal system when voicing one's views.

The great documentary photographers since the dawn of photo-journalism, the likes of Henri Cartier-Bresson, Robert Capa and Sir Don McCullin had always taken an objective interest in their subjects. The documentary photo is less to do with perfect exposure, composition or to meet the aesthetic ideals of what generally constitutes a 'good' photo. It is more about being in the moment and capturing the essence of the moment with the greatest sympathy. Cartier-Bresson coined a term, 'the decisive moment,' which in itself, has sparked many academic volumes, lectures and seminars over the last sixty years. That decisive moment can't be self-generated by the photographer, all he or she could do in the old days was to set the camera lens aperture to f8, select a hyper-focal distance allowing for the maximum possibility of the main subject being in focus, and press the shutter button, hence another coined phrase: 'f8 and be there.' Despite the technological leaps made in the functioning of the camera, 'be there' remains a truthful mantra for the documentary photographer, whatever camera is used to tell the story.

The poet Wilfred Owen wrote about WWI as a first-hand participant. Other observer-participants were his fellow soldiers—carrying their vest-pocket Kodak cameras. Such photos from the trenches were banned by the War Office, especially once newspapers started to pay soldiers for a more realistic depiction of their experiences. These were never formally commissioned photos, but highly sought after. The War Office eventually commissioned artists as secondary observers to portray a less visceral and gruesome version of the war.

I, of course, have never worked in a war zone and have no ambition to do so. Nor have I formally worked for a publication or had been commissioned to cover a story, which is what the professional photojournalist had traditionally relied upon as far as the economics of the career went. I had to make do with my fine-art portraiture and weddings, and so, sadly, there came the time when I just didn't have the time to attend even the big protests.

With the demise of local newspapers and the advent of phone cameras, the specialist freelance photographer is increasingly being replaced by the citizen photojournalist. So, if the thrill alone did not pull me to a protest or the joy of sharing the photos to a wide social media group, sadly, there is no other recompense. Presently, the largest of Welsh rallies would typically be photographed by freelance photojournalists, photography students and in some instances—if it is 'considered' to be of mainstream interest—a television journalist may turn up! Following the rally, all freelance photojournalists would rush home or to the nearest high-speed internet café to upload a selection of the photos to their agencies.

For me, the reflective moments really began at the editing stage, when I'd select the best ten to fifteen photos that tell the story in the way I would want to tell a story. The protest is the main story but how do I tell the story within, which story am I telling? And in most cases, which story is likely to find a buyer from the shrinking band of print publications or the plethora of online publications who might be looking for a free photo snapped by a someone present at the event? These remain the questions for anyone filing their montage to send to an agency or photo editor.

There are also other considerations: social media sharing, for example, who are the core participants at T.S. Eliot's 'hot gates,' who now have as much a right to be included in the story—however bland a storyline a particular photo might serve. I started to notice that if I missed the photos of certain acquaintances, the Facebook un-friend button was all too near! This has often made me wonder whether the inner conflict of wanting to be acknowledged as part of a movement by the activist is just as great as the cause itself. I have often felt like that old man from 'Gerontion' at protest rallies—a non-combatant, camera in hand, rather than a placard.

To me, 'Gerontion' is not about the moralising of triumph of good over evil, but merely looking at the brutality of conflict in a way that chides the concept of heroism. The moral maxim confronting the purpose of 'doing good,' or making amends for past bad, is questionable. Gerontion literally means an old man and like most old men, the narrator has regrets. One of the principal regrets is for reasons not spelled out in the poem, he was not at the 'hot gates.' This allusion to the battle of Thermopylae (480 BC) between the Ancient Greeks and Persians, and 'nor knee deep in salt marsh', a refence to his non-participation in WW1, the old man is merely stating that he did not actively participate in some of the most significant conflicts during his life. However, there is an active realisation that conflicts never truly go away, because the struggle for establishing political ideals, whether through war, politics, or protest marches, is perpetual. WWII was a direct result of the unresolved grievances and a sense of humiliation felt by the losing side in WWI. The 'cold war', long painted as a struggle between capitalism and communism was in turn a direct result of the political and economic forces that emerged following WWII.

I strongly feel that the direct results of conflicts between the good and evil or light and dark, as often propagated through religious and political fanaticism, is what T.S. Eliot cites as 'history has many cunning passages'. Later in life, Eliot converted to Anglicanism, but the fascination with Eastern religious traditions, where a 'dualistic' worldview is the accepted norm, can be found in many of his poems including the monumental *Four Quartets*.

Having documented successive political protests, activism, and dissent over a period of time, I have come to conclude that activism shall always remain central to human existence. In a dualistic view of the world, perhaps something similar to what is found in the ancient religious traditions of Zoroastrianism and Manichaeism, the presence of darkness is accepted and is deemed important, because it makes us appreciate the light more. Perhaps, activism and the desire to fight for any cause is a subconscious acceptance of that dualistic view of competing forces, and the activist is always at the 'hot gates', standing up for injustices?

Fionn Wilson, *Building on Fire* (2016)

Child *A Speech*

By Sierra Moulinié

I am the child
of a system of government
so corrupt that families
starve, or beg, or steal,
because a parent's benefits
have been sanctioned
after they were too sick
for a pointless meeting,
whilst billionaires and CEOs
are allowed to keep doing
anything they want,
simply because they went
to schools with fancy ties
and silly handshakes.

I am the child
of a society so heartless
that people will step over
a weeping woman lying
in the filthy gutter,
or avert their gazes
from a shamefaced man
who begs for some money
to feed his starving children,
just because they have been
taught that these people
aren't really people,
and to be looked down on,
spat on, and despised.

I am the child
of a world so full of hate
that tyrants and demagogues
are applauded for actions
like using flimsy excuses
to justify dropping bombs
on schools and hospitals
or as a reason to send
countless young people
to die in needless crusades
just because they're offended
at the name of another god,
or to fill their pockets with
blood money and kickbacks
from the people who made
the bombs that they're dropping.

I am the child
of a culture so poisoned
by arbitrary distrust and fear
that we close our borders
and slash our aid budgets
even as our actions worldwide
do nothing but grow
the tide of refugees fleeing
from their shattered homelands,
and where our children
are taught to regard others
as terrorists and murderers
just because their skin
is a shade darker than ours?

I am the child
of a world that needs to change.

Gustavius Payne, *The Passion*

if what I have to say offends you ...

By Summar Jade

...now before I go off on an explosive rant please note I do understand that not all men are like this. not all men treat women this way. but it happens so often that us women, that we have built up this perception of men due to our shitty experiences, so who can blame us when we say *all men are the same* because most men we meet, treat us like shit. and even the nice ones break your trust. those finite hairs of trust have been snapped on so many occasions ... so much so, that I feel bald. a scalped integrity where words once grew.

instead, I am

enraged by the fact that men feel they have the right to comment on my body in a negative way ... tell us we're too fat, or too thin,

your nipples are too big,
your pussy isn't tight enough.
I prefer blondes.
why did you dye your hair?
your skin is too bare.
you have too many tattoos.
I wish you dressed more slutty.
I wish you would cover up, more.

what if I told a man that his penis was small? he'd be enraged, I'm sure. why does he have the right to express his anger, yet a woman has to take it with grace? I've even had one man tell me that if they are going to have sex with me then I better shave my pussy. I didn't even bother replying, I wrote a poem about it instead and called it 'NO!' on a train from swansea to llanelli I had a drunk man smack my bum. lucky I'm outspoken. lucky I'm disobedient, because I decided in that moment to grab him by his neck and asked him if he thought he has a right to touch me. I was lucky there was a full carriage of people. if I was alone, I wouldn't have been as brave.

I was dating a guy a few years back. he was 5 years older. we had been using condoms during sex and after us being together for a few weeks, I went and got myself checked out. it came back I had chlamydia, so I went to have a chat with him about this as I thought it was the responsible thing to do. I told him he should be alright as we have been using condoms, but he should go get checked, just in case ... and I explained the medication was simple to take, and *it's gone before you know it.* instead of being like *aw, cool, sucks I gotta go get checked but thanks for the heads up.* no! he called me dirty. I asked if he had ever been checked and he said, *I've never needed to, I've trusted my partners.* I tried to explain that trust doesn't prevent chlamydia. but he would rather call me *dirty* and judge me, than ever consider he might have something himself. it's a well-known fact that men are the carriers of chlamydia as they display less or barely any symptoms.

I was in the early days of a relationship and I told my partner from the start that I wasn't interested in being degraded or humiliated during sex... that's a no-go for me. he asked me multiple times to *throat fuck* me or to *fuck my head* as he was fascinated in doing that kind of thing. that guy was a whole book of red flags. I didn't love myself enough to know better at the time. we live and learn fortunately.

but this isn't just personal, it's historical. my ancestors went through the same, and worse, so why do we keep making excuses for shitty behaviour?

this isn't anyone-in-particulars fault. so if what I have to say offends you, you're missing the point. I'm sure whoever is reading this has felt oppression and in its many forms, and what I have to say is that my oppressor is your oppressor too.

Rachel Oliver, *Do Not Fear Your Fear*

COVID-39

By Xavier Panadès i Blas

She ran, ran, and ran... Her eyes flashed desperately searching for a place to feint. She sped through the hairpin turns of the alleys of Old Abertawe, as if the hordes of Hell were chasing her. She saw shadow instead of a door and stepped into a disused portal.

Her breath was condensing in front of her in the cool morning air. Cautiously, she glanced back from where she had come from hiding. No one was following her. She was aware that she was naked in the face of death. His chest throbbed, sweat running down his back from the effort. It would only save her coming home undetected.

The mask had suddenly been blown off in the middle of David John Williams Square. People avoided her like an elephant defecating in a tiny room. They didn't even look at her. The social silence reigned so intensely that I heard the screeching of the multiple digital eyes, which they relentlessly watched over the population.

Since COVID-23 ten years ago, states had imposed extraordinary measures to stop new strains of the virus. People always had to wear masks and could not speak in public.

Everyone had been forced to microchip their ears and have weekly COVID tests. Disobeying them, or helping the one who broke them, led to the immediate elimination of the individual and / or individuals.

She only lived three blocks away. She took a deep breath. She made a mind map and chose a route between alleys where there was little surveillance. It was a bit longer, but much safer.

She took one last look at the alley. Empty. She ran as fast as she could and rounded the corner; smiled. The front door of her house was less than a minute away. Climb the stone stairs, cross the main street and the guardian dragon tattooed on the portal would welcome you.

She ran to the end of the alley. She darted up the three flights of stairs and hurried toward the dragon... Suddenly, she felt a heat on her back that spread to the rest of her body. It lulled her sweetly. Without pain, she totally lost consciousness.

Leaning against the wall, she reflected on listening to the early morning birdsong of the city as her life literally slipped away. Blood ran in rivers between the pebbles from the wound on her chest. As her body grew weak, she watched the light slowly fade from her eyes.

Catalan Translation

Corría, corría, y corría ... Sus ojos centelleaban desesperadamente buscando un lugar donde amagarse. Aceleraba por las curvas cerradas de los callejones del casco antiguo de Abertawe, como si las hordas del infierno la estuvieran persiguiendo. Vio sombra en lugar de una puerta y se metió en un portal en desuso.

Su respiración se condensaba frente a ella en el aire fresco de la mañana. Con cautela, miró hacia atrás desde su escondite por donde había venido. Nadie la seguía. Era consciente de que estaba desnuda frente a la muerte. Su pecho palpitaba, el sudor le corría por la espalda por el esfuerzo. Solo la salvaría llegar a su hogar sin ser detectada.

La máscara se le había volado repentinamente en medio de la plaza David John Williams. La gente la evitaba como un elefante defecando en una habitación minúscula. Ni la miraban. El silencio social imperaba tan intensamente, que oía el chirrir de los múltiples ojos digitales, que vigilaban implacablemente.

Desde la COVID-23 diez años atrás, los estados habían impuesto unas medidas extraordinarias hasta nuevo aviso para detener las nuevas cepas del virus. La gente siempre debía llevar máscara y no podía hablar en público.

Todo el mundo había sido forzado a insertarse un microchip en la oreja y a hacerse pruebas semanales de COVID. Desobedecerlas, o ayudar al que las rompía, llevaba a eliminar al individuo y/o individuos inmediatamente.

Solo vivía a tres calles. Inspiró profundamente. Hizo un mapa mental y escogió una ruta entre callejones donde había poca vigilancia. Era un trayecto un poco más largo, pero mucho más seguro.

Echó un último vistazo al callejón. Vacío. Corrió lo más rápido que pudo y dobló la esquina; sonrió. La puerta principal de su casa estaba a menos de un minuto. Subir las escaleras de piedra, cruzar la calle principal y el dragón gaudiano tatuado en el portal le daría la bienvenida.

Corrió hasta el final de la callejuela. Subió como una flecha los tres tramos de escaleras y se apresuró hacia el dragón... Repentinamente, notó un calor en su espalda que se extendió al resto de su cuerpo. La adormecía dulcemente. Sin dolor, perdió totalmente el conocimiento.

Adosada a la pared, reflexionó sobre escuchar el canto de los pájaros de la madrugada de la ciudad, mientras literalmente su vida se esfumaba. La sangre corría en ríos entre los guijarros de la herida en su pecho. Mientras su cuerpo se debilitaba, vio cómo la luz se desvanecía lentamente de sus ojos.

Alzó la cabeza lentamente y sonrió dulcemente a la imagen de su madre dándole la bienvenida. El olor de las manzanas recién cocidas, con que le daba la bienvenida, la expurgaba del dolor físico de dejar el mundo de los vivos.

Un zumbido mecánico comenzó a moverse hacia ella. Era irregular como si el dron mostrara frustración a pesar de haberla cazado. ¿No le gustó que transcendiera su mundo felizmente? Fue la última pregunta antes de desvanecerse de aquel mundo deshumanizado.

Previously published in Castilian at Benma Editores (Mexico).

Extract from 'Norte'

By Jon Gower

There are precious few pleasures in the lives of Juan Pablo and his sister Carmena. Neither of them has ever received a present or a toy. Too many days have been and gone without their having anything for supper other than some sugar mixed with water, creating the illusion of food without being food, a treachery on the tongue. But the syrup is never enough to stop the clenching of the stomach, the griping like a cold snake turning and turning deep within the innards. The sugar turning wormwood.

Night after night of starvation. By now the two children have learned not to expect much when their mother returns from the streets, where she has been selling tortillas, or bundles of old clothes, or individual cigarettes. They can only pray that she hasn't sold each and every one tortilla.

The family wasn't always this poor. When their father lived with them they had a little bit of money and Juan Pablo was the most popular pupil in Escuela 23, not because of anything to do with him but rather to do with his father's job, as he was an animal trapper.

In the old days, when the economy and the peso were weaker, Juan Pablo's father would trap to order on behalf of many of the world's zoos— Berlin, San Diego, the Bois de Boulogne in Paris—and the sum he'd receive for, say, an ocelot or a fer de lanse would be pretty reasonable, even though, as his father would often aver, wasn't *everything* in Latin America cheap and reasonable? A whole continent begging on its knees, as he would like to describe it, after one too many mescals down the cantina. 'Pleez Señor America, can you give us a dollar for our skins? Two for our daughters? Three for our allegiance to your flag.'

Because Juan Pablo had a house full of animals everyone wanted to be his friend, and on those days when his father's truck cloud-dusted up the road on returning from a hunting trip every kid in the neighbourhood wanted to be on hand to see what wriggling goodies he'd brought home.

He would empty his cargo into jars, cages and occasionally into a corral, should he have been lucky enough to snaffle some substantial animal or other, constantly playing tricks as he did so. He would describe pretty much every snake he unloaded as 'the most dangerous in the whole, wide world' before hurling it in the direction of the hysterical kids, who would squeal and run even though they knew that this was only a trick and that this gentle man wouldn't ever harm them in truth.

But gradually the big orders dwindled and Juan Pablo's dad had to re-direct his efforts, collecting on behalf of smaller outfits, tawdry zoos scattered around Central America, where a tapir was worth no more than 10,000 pesos, no matter how much time he had taken to trap it. Thank God for the private, obsessive collectors in the Estados Unidos who still paid over the odds for some rare beast. Like the trillionaire in Huston who delighted in amassing species that were on the edge of extinction. So he could cook them and eat them. People are strange. The money for those would go straight into an account in the Caiman Islands.

One day his father gave Juan Pablo a macaw which already had a small vocabulary. Arbol. A tree. Amor. Love. Texas. This was to be the last present before his father disappeared. Perhaps to Texas. Perhaps not. Juan Pablo never found out where he went, or what had happened to him. He did not know about his father plunging to his death off a cliff when hunting Gila monsters for a wealthy client in Tokyo.

Juan never stopped guessing what had happened. Running away with another woman? Having other kids in Wichita or Rochelle or Yuba City? Drinking away the money he was meant to send home? It would be a blessing to know how his father died.

Hunting.

Trying to provide, to earn some precious money for the family he loved like breath.

Extract from 'Norte'
(Welsh translation)

Prin yw'r pleserau ym mywydau Juan Pablo a'i chwaer Carmena. Nid yw'r un o'r ddau erioed wedi cael anrheg na thegan go iawn, ac mae gormod o ddyddiau wedi mynd a dod heb ddim i swper ar wahân i siwgr wedi ei gymysgu â dŵr, i greu argraff o fwyd, i dwyllo'r tafod. Ond nid yw hyn yn ddigon i roi stop ar wingo'r stumog, y ffordd mae'n teimlo fel neidr oer yn troi a throi a throelli'n rhywle'n ddwfn yn yr ymysgaroedd. Y siwgr yn troi'n wermwd.

Noson ar ôl noson o newynu. Erbyn hyn, mae'r ddau blentyn wedi dysgu peidio â disgwyl llawer pan mae eu mam wedi bod allan ar y strydoedd yn gwerthu *tortillas*, ney fwndel o hen ddillad, neu sigaréts unigol, allan nhw ddim ond gweddïo nad yw hi wedi gwerthu pob un o'r *tortillas*.

Nid oedd y teulu wastad mor dlawd â hyn. Pan oedd ei tad yn byw gyda nhw, roedd ganddyn nhw ychydig bach o arian, a Juan Pablo oedd y bachgen mwyaf poblogaidd yn Escuela 23, nid o'i herwydd ei hunan odn oherwydd gwaith ei dad, oedd yn drapiwr anifeiliaid.

Yn yr hen ddyddiau, pan oedd yr *economia* a'r peso yn wan, byddai tad Juan Pablo'n trapio ar ran rhai o sŵs mwyaf y byd—Berlin, San Diego, y Bois de Boulogne ym Mharis—a byddai'r pris am bob oselot neu *fer de lanse* neu ta beth yn rhesymol iawn, er, fel y byddai tad Juan Pablo'n dadlau byth a beunydd, onid oedd *popeth* yn America Ladin yn tsiep a rhesymol? Cyfandir cyfan yn cardota, fel y byddai'n ei ddweud ar ôl cael llon croen o *mezcal* yn y *cantina*. 'Pleeze Señor America, can you give us a dollar for our skins? Two for our daughters? Three for our allegiance to the flag?'

Ond oherwydd bod gan Juan Pablo lond tŷ o anifeiliaid, roedd pawb am fod yn ffrind iddo, ac ar y diwrnodau hynny pan fyddai cerbyd ei dad yn dod lan yr hewl mewn cwmwl o ddwst ar ôl bod i ffwrdd ar un o'i dripiau hela, byddai pob plentyn yr yr ardal yn aros yn eiddgar amdano yn un dorf fawr.

Byddai'n arllwys cynhwysion y tryc i jariau, cewyll ac ambell i gorâl ar gyfer yr anifeiliaid mwy sylweddol, gan chwarae triciau wrth iddo wneud. Byddai'n disgrifio bron pob neidr fel yr un fwyaf peryglus yn y byd ac yn ffugio lluchio'r sarff i gyfeiriad y plant, fyddai'n gwichian mewn ofn er bod y rhan fwyaf yn gwybod mai tric oedd e, ac na fyddai'r gŵr addfwyn hwn yn eu peryglu.

Ond yn raddol, edwinodd yr archebion mawr a bu'n rhaid iddo

arallgyfeirio, gan gasglu i sŵs bach llwm mewn llefydd diarffordd, dwstlyd ar draws America Ganol, lle byddai tapir yn gwerthu am ddim mwy na 10,000 *peso*, waeth pa mor hir y byddai wedi gymryd i'w ddal. Diolch byth am y casglwyr preifat, obsesiynol yn America oedd yn fodlon talu crocbris am greaduriaid prin. Fel y *trillionaire* yn Houston oedd yn arbenigo mewn casglu rhywogaethau oedd ar fin mynd i ddifodiant. Er mwyn eu coginio a'u bwyta. Mae pobl yn rhyfedd. Byddai'r arian yn dod yn syth i'w gyfrif o fanc yn Ynysoedd y Caiman.

Un diwrnod, rhoddodd ei dad facáw i Juan Pablo, a oedd yn medru ynganu ambell air yn barod. *Árbol*. Coeden. *Amor*. Cariad. Tecsas. Hon oedd yn anrheg olaf. Diflannodd ei dad. Efallai i Decsas. Efallai ddim. Ni ddaeth Juan Pablo byth i wybod beth ddigwyddodd i'w dad. Ni wyddai mae syrthio oddi ar glogwyn wrth geisio dal tri Gila i gwsmer cyfoethog yn Tokyo wnaeth e, druan. Weithiau, roedd yn ceisio dyfalu beth fu ei hanes. Rhedeg i ffwrdd gyda menyw arall? Cael plant eraill lan yn Wichita neu Rochelle neu Yuba City? Yfed yr arian roedd yn bwriadu ei anfon adref? O, byddai'n dda petai e'n gwybod mai fel hyn y bu farw ei dad. Yn hela. Yn ceisio ennill arian i'w deulu, yr un yr oedd yn ei garu fel anadl.

Alan Perry, *Homeless Man*

Industry in the Country of the Blind

By Rob Mimpriss

'Three hundred miles and more from Chimborazo, one hundred from the snows of Cotopaxi...'
—H. G. Wells.

There is a sculpture outside the train station which serves the Country of the Blind. Cast in bronze, it shows the valley's discoverer, standing almost at the crest of a crag with a young woman by his side. He gazes southward, past the station towards the mountains into which he made his escape, one hand raised to shield his eyes from the sun, the other holding the woman's arm in guidance or support. The woman, bare footed, is nursing a child, her face is turned towards the ground, while surrounding them both is a sea of uplifted hands, grasping their ankles in supplication or treachery. A plaque in Roman script and Braille commemorates their names, Ricardo Núñez and Medina-Saroté, his lover, after whom the town is named.

The statue is regularly vandalised, and as regularly repaired. The nationalists, the Serenos, paint their slogans over the plinth or hammer them into the bronze in a kind of inverse Braille; they lock fetters round the wrists of those upturned hands, or they cover Núñez's eyes with goats' blood as though they have been gouged. The staff in the tourist cafés whose glass fronts line the square will disavow the Serenos. They are not from Medina-Saroté, they will claim, but from Las Piñas or Cien Fuegos to the north; they are blind and come to Medina-Saroté to drink their disability pensions; they are fanatics, who have hijacked the cultural heritage of the Valley as a pretext for their hate. In some of the cafés a few blocks to the north, or on the pavement outside the Casa Rosada where there are poetry readings on Thursday nights, the condemnations will seem more measured. Enucleation is a thing of the past, people will say, just as forced labour is a thing of the past. Because of gold, Núñez enslaved the people and broke their ways, and because of gold, they are building the old ways again. Perhaps some waiter will take a liking to you. He will mention *Senderisma*, the philosophy of the Ways, he will direct you to one of the bookshops, or the museum. He will suggest you take one of the walking tours of the perimeter wall or the parts of the Ways that have been restored; he will smile in dismissal or touch your arm as he peers at you in the sunlight.

When Ricardo Núñez discovered the valley, the ways ran the full forty-seven miles from the meadows where Medina-Saroté stands to the rocky landscape of the far north, intersecting and meeting to form a grid which every male child began to memorise as soon as he could walk. Alongside the goat-bells and the plough, the bagpipes and alpenhorns, the milk churns and butter presses and simple children's toys, the museum displays a man's letter-staff and a woman's girdle with the Ways encoded in knot-work. A piece of old film, digitised and displayed in cycle on a screen, shows the Valley's last cantor, Enrique González, sitting in a windowless room as he chants the ways and their waymarks, their landmarks and their natural histories, a complete cosmography of the Blind. The gift shop sells fragments of the old chants set to ambient music, walkers' and bird-watchers' guides, and books on *senderisma*. Buy a book from the woman behind the counter who has watched you browsing with goat-like eyes. It will be something to read on the way.

The visiting lecturer at Cardiff University is an exile from the Valley, nicknamed The Cord. He sits on the podium, a tanned, spare man with a powerful brow and eye-sockets in shadow and declines when invited to come forward to the podium, giving his lecture still seated, his head turned a little sideways as he reads from the letter-staff in his hand. The lecture is a curious network of accidents and associations: the discovery of coal in the Rhondda, and Ricardo Núñez's discovery of gold; Maredudd Ddall, the captive prince sent home to Wales blinded by Henry II, and Núñez's Breaking of the Ways; the Welsh Not; Wounded Knee, and the text that Núñez had carved on the hand-rails that guided his slaves through the mines: In the Country of the Blind, every man is a king.

The landslide that enwombed his people in their valley came about by accident, without warning, just as Núñez's arrival was so unexpected that they concluded that he had been born of the rocks. But the thin air and fierce light that caused the settlers to go blind, and the genetic quirk by means of which they were eventually born without eyes, made themselves felt over generations, so that his ancestors had time to prepare. When Núñez came among them, they had adapted to life without sight; they had built the wall that protected their meadows from rockfalls, and the system of roads that forms the Wayland, the *Matriz*, so that when Núñez and the prospectors and mercenaries who came with him opened the mines at Cien Fuegos, their slaves were able to learn and navigate its tunnels as easily as they had moved around the valley above their heads.

The history of the Wayland can be told as the elevation of a disability into the basis of a culture, and the degradation of that culture into a disability. The achievements of the Blind as a people are the Ways as a means of giving shape to the land, the knot-work girdle and the letter-staff as systems of writing, and the chants of the cantors as philosophy and literature; while their humiliation is expressed in the disability cheques that they draw from the government every week, the televisions that they buy, yet cannot watch, their widespread reliance on alcohol; yet the humiliation begins in Núñez's time, and in his mines. The slave-workers who died there died for gold, a metal that has no value except to the sight, whose very name is the name of its colour, so that the foremen tormented their slaves with the taunt that they could never even know why they must die. During the uprising at Cien Fuegos, seven captured foremen were blinded in the town square, and left to grope their way home to their blind wives as best they could. And when Medina-Saroté gave birth to Núñez's son, she gouged out his eyes so that he would never succumb to that cruel and grasping madness called sight.

Souvenirs for the tourists

Senderisma, an attitude of staying on the Ways, of understanding oneself as a part of the cosmos. A reliance on the knowledge of the Ways that one has been taught, bringing with it a sense of respect for one's forebears and kinship with one's neighbours, and an obligation to help maintain the Ways without which one is lost. As you read your book, the bus takes the modern road north-east, following the former route of Núñez's railroad, past modern houses with bay windows facing south; past retail parks and hayfields; past a village of blank stone walls where a wide-eyed child guides her grandfather on to the bus, his eye-sockets shadowed by the rim of his hat; past a water-bottling plant and a private spa, until jettied houses of black pinewood and grey stone show that you are entering Las Piñas, and the driver turns the engine off outside the Longhouse in the main square.

The valley narrows here. A mountain ridge covered with pine forests runs down to meet the river, and where the air is filled with the roar of waterfalls and the rumbling of the glaciers, Ricardo Núñez made his home, and later adventurers founded a sanatorium or two. There are guided tours. The oldest of the blind guides, known as The Goat, will take you up through pine forests to listen to the songs of the birds which once, he explained, were revered as the Spirits of the Air, towards that mingling of forest and scree where Núñez dismantled the boundary wall to use the stone for his building. The Longhouse offers a benefits office, a public library, legal advice; signs brightly painted on wood in the square point the way to river rafting, hostels and bunkhouses, restaurants, forest walks. There is a tourists' office on the other side of the square. A relief map shows the mountains surrounding the Valley, the three main towns, and sections of wall. Other displays, and much of the merchandise, represent the wildlife of the Valley and the folklore of the Blind, especially concerning their national hero, Hernando.

Hernando, guided by the Spirits of the Air, taught the people to clear their pastures of the stones and use the stones to build their houses. Hernando, inspired by the Spirits of the Air, taught the people to bell their goats, so that wherever they wandered, they could find them. Hernando followed the riverbank south from Cien Fuegos, gathering pebbles as he went, until the sound of the river was the sound of his home, and he knew that he was at Las Piñas. Hernando called his name and the name of his farmstead, as the custom was, and let shouted voices guide him, but once home, he did not rest. He called out his name and the name of his neighbours until they called him in, leaving pebbles from the river behind him on the way, and so the first of the Ways was laid from farmstead to farmstead, from man to man.

As Hernando grew older, he came to understand that he would not always be with the people to defend or guide them, and so he appointed cantors to travel the ways and teach the people the chants, and he took the strongest men once again and set them the task of building the wall. When it was finished, it stood so tall that a man could barely reach the top of it with his arms up stretched, and its foundations were as deep as a man's feet are from his chest, and it circled the valley from its southern tip to the furthest north and back again, so that there was nowhere for the Men of the Rocks to break through. When the work was done, Hernando departed from his people and was reconciled with the Spirits of the Air, but if they care for the wall and keep to the paths, the people can be sure that he hears them and keeps the Wayland safe.

Who hears the Blind today, asks the Cord; who keeps the Wayland safe? The way from Cien Fuegos to its seat of government is the way of the sighted young when they leave: by bus through Las Piñas to Medina-Sarote, by train through the tunnel gouged through the mountains to bring Núñez's workers to the mines and export Núñez's gold, to San Martin or Puente Angosto where they will be told that if they are looking for work, there is no work there, and they must go on to the capital city, where one could sit for a year in the legislature without hearing the Wayland mentioned.

Could the people of the Wayland rebuild the Ways? The Blind and ill-sighted who stay in the valley have their disability payments, their drugs and alcohol, their sense of themselves and their history as an accident and a curse. They can pick up work in the craft shops making souvenirs, or as tour guides in the gold mines; they can join the Serenos to firebomb some new hotel or deface a statue or two. Others know that if it is pointless to fight, it is pointless also to debate. For if we speak of the dignity of the Blind, we are heard to be calling for enucleations; if we speak of the heritage of the *Matriz*, we are accused of rejecting all progress. It was after the blinding of the foremen in Cien Fuegos that Núñez broke the Ways. He tore up the waymarks, he flattened the verges, he heaped the ways with slag from his mines and laid landmines made by his slaves, not merely to take ownership of the valley or isolate the people, but to break their spirit. Yet *Senderisma* and the stories of Hernando commodify and infantilise the Wayland's culture to serve the tourist trade, while Medina-Sarote, blinding her child, becomes a rebuke to those who reject the state's view of progress. That the sighted must protect and care for the blind, who in Núñez's case protected and cared for the sighted, becomes proof that our heritage is a weakness and a burden, just as here in this national capital the language is cited as proof that you are unworthy to be a nation, that to desire to be so is divisive and backward, proof of a sickness of mind.

As the bus heads north from Las Piñas it begins to rain. The driver plays light classics, and the family in front of you eat chorizo and hard-boiled eggs as the bright light of the mountains dims under heavy cloud, and the road passes straight through sombre alps and past windowless farmhouses crouched in the shelter of spruce trees. You stop at Agua Sucia, and the road begins to climb. Pastures give way to moorlands heaped with slag tips and checked with polluted streams; the valley begins to die in a chaos of gorge and ridge, and glaciers grey with soot rise above chimneystacks venting flame. There is a smell. Something thick in the air catches the throat. Disembark at the bus station and walk through snow and rain past the law court and the police station, up windowless streets, past the blind feeling their way with their sticks as the sighted young slouch past them, past loan companies, past vendors of repossessed goods, past a Pentecostal church where the Blind are promised sight, towards the memorial in the main square where the foremen were blinded.

    The figures are cast in bronze on a shallow plinth. Two lines of seven are depicted walking barefoot over broken ground, those behind with their hands on the leaders' shoulders, the blind with their eye-sockets covered over with flesh, the blinded wrapped in rags where their eyes have been gouged out.

    Steps behind them lead onto the plinth. To the side, modern shoes are cast in bronze, and you take the hint, bending down to undo your laces so that like the statues themselves you will walk barefoot. The rough bronze will bruise your feet. You will likely trip. You will put out a hand for support.

Arron Kuiper, *Wales & Rebellion*

The Princes of Mynydd Dinas

By Philip John

"Are you coming up the mountain today?" asked Gerallt, with a glint of adventure in his eye. And so we rode on invisible horseback with our wooden swords aloft and made our way up into those barren hills of home. Before we ascended, we galloped through an underpass just before the foothills. We saw the pieces of lost hope that young princes can barely recognise. Scattered paraphernalia was narrated by the graffiti on the wall —not a war paint warning but just the helpless cries of another generation failed by the system.

Before we entered into battle with the princes of the other valleys, we had time enough to gaze beyond the curtain of summer's heat and cast our youthful eyes beyond the ragged edges of Mynydd Dinas. An old colliery, in slumber for some time, gazed back at us with warning eyes. Our forefathers had told us many tales of times gone by—the days and nights they dug for the diamonds of black and their children who dug for some more. They had worked on and on for a pittance, for to barely be fed and clothed.

The echoes of our old language are sung from a chapel nearby and the sweet sound of their swansong sends us into battle to fight for a better life than them. The clatter of the swords and the jeers of the warriors on the mound will all be lost in legends, a far cry away from the glory of a childhood in the green of the valley.

Gerallt, my compatriot, loses himself in the battle and he rolls amongst the ferns in desperation—a fallen prince in the fields of destiny. I tried my best to steady him as he fumbled his way back down the rocky slopes of life. That day I thought he'd live to fight another but instead he shuffled away—forever in his thoughts. Through the long and winding slivers of steep terraced streets that snake their way from top to bottom, I see his ghost still wandering and lost in broken dreams.

The young prince is now a pirate and he deals in pills and powders; he's buying and he's selling and he'll blight this place he calls home. I feel torn about what to make of what became of him—he was not gifted with stability, and all our opportunities went up in the smoke of the lost industry.

Desire was lost in the black clouds of adolescence and the pathway to a better tomorrow replaced by one less travelled by. The time came for me to mount the horse once more and I rode out into exile to find out what more to life there could be.

Many Rhondda sunsets have sunk into the valley since I rode away, and many men and women were forced to ride out of there as well. I travelled many lands beyond the border and sailed beyond the seas that serve as walls. How enlightening it was to see what we could become and just how far we have to go. No more time to be victims of circumstance nor dependents to the colonial invaders of the past, but onwards we must go to forge a better way ahead and a renewal once again.

A cultural awakening has already begun and the dragon was only sleeping—the Cymraeg rolls from its tongue and roars like thunder from its heart. Yet the fight for social justice and a better way ahead is a prophecy yet to be fulfilled—the struggle wages on. So when I march through home again I want to bring the truth and *Y Mab Darogan*'s force for change. Wake up, Wales, wake up! The princes of Mynydd Dinas are ready to be kings!

Sarah Oneill, *Pit Pony*

Be the Best

By Jon Doyle

W‍e'd never played Ely before, but we'd heard about them. Our old men laughed and winced when we mentioned the name. "They don't fuck about up there boys," they warned. We tried to imagine. We put it out of our minds. We beat Porthcawl and Port Talbot and Kenfig Hill and went within one win of having the best start our side had ever managed. But then we had to go to Ely. Ely boys carried knives, is what we'd heard.

*

"Everyone on?" Coach asked as he started the engine. Coach's voice was always croaky, and our theory was that he lived alone and didn't speak to anyone during the week. It might have been true. He spent weekends with us after all, surely not his first choice in life.

The bus had a CD player and the boys had CDs—mixes of radio rock and techno that they'd ripped from Limewire and burned to disc.

"My brother's got a secret site," Wormy shouted over the music. "Can get anything you want. Music, games, porn."

"What about *Civilisation* then?" Titch asked. "I asked for that like three weeks ago."

"You never said which one," Wormy yelled back. "I told you that. There's *Civilisation I, Civilisation II*. My brother can get them all."

The song playing sounding like a jackhammer on fast forward.

"Oi, we picking Alex up today?" Alien wanted to know.

Alien got his nickname on account of the shape of his head, but no-one gave him shit about it anymore.

"Yes," Coach said.

"Well we just drove past him."

Coach swore and looked for somewhere to turn. I felt bad for Coach, but never knew how to show it.

Alex stood waiting with his hand down his joggers. The minibus door was a fucker to open, and we could never do it. It pissed Coach off no end because it meant he had to get out and open it for us. He could do it easy. Had the knack.

"Alright?" "Alright?" "Alright?" said the boys as Alex climbed aboard. "Alright?" he said back.

Alex worked night shifts every Friday and Saturday at a building supplies warehouse down by the docks, moving sacks of sand and cement from one pile to another and sometimes back again. He got off at seven and a feller drop him by the junction, boots and shinpads in a *Happy Shopper* bag. The job was his father's idea, to give him a taste of the Real World. Alex seemed to have accepted his fate and he scared us half to death.

The CD skipped aggressively, a malfunction or part of the song that sounded like how I imagined a stroke might feel.

"Ready to get stabbed, son?" Woody shouted.

Slinging his bag into the aisle and taking a seat, Alex didn't look much bothered either way.

*

That week in school, the Army had come in. Trying to get us to Be The Best. They brought a couple of dickheads in combat fatigues and a climbing wall and had us doing army stuff all morning. Marching and trying on helmets and that. They even had a gun, a big black SA80-something, but we didn't reckon it was real.

In the afternoon we went into the assembly hall and listened to talks by army people. The chef, the engineer, the dentist. The middle-aged officer who spoke of the glory of the Royal Welsh and fielded questions about slug sizes and headshots. They projected a slideshow on the wall. Soldiers in ghillie suits, soldiers in swamps, scowling soldiers in formation like a well-oiled machine. The young men in the pictures either looked like they wanted to be your mate or kill you, and those operating the biggest guns looked back out of frame as though to check their bosses, or maybe their fathers, were watching.

At the end of the day, they set up a table by the door with a sign-up sheet. They called it a Declaration of Interest form. You had to pass them to get out the door, and in the queue, we joked about terrorists and the Taliban. When I got closer my heart started hammering and I felt sick as hell even though I knew I could walk right past. I was going to be the first Sullivan to go to university. I didn't need the Army.

I put my name down anyway, and it was weird. Nothing changed. I went to the vending machine and grabbed a *Coke* and *Kit Kat* and I walked out of the school gates just the same.

*

The CD staggered on to some arena band and Boycey argued with Ashley about who was better—these or Slipknot. Ash loved Slipknot and all that. Boycey said they were for autistics and school shooters.

There were too many of us on the bus now. The sign above the door said MAXIMUM CAPACITY: 15 but we'd picked up Dean Perry and the Dale twins and they had to sit on the floor in the aisle.

Poor fucking Perry was always having to do shit like that. Someone told me he slept top-and-tail with his brother because they didn't have enough bedrooms. We'd gone to his house once to get him, and Coach made me and Woody get out and knock. His mother asked us in and it turned out his entire living room was full of cages. Budgies, hamsters, gerbils, he had them all. Guinea pigs, rats, a parrot that said *I don't believe it* like that old fella from TV. It didn't smell great in there. Not like shit or anything, but not great. Mrs Perry was still in her dressing gown and looked mighty pissed off at something, but she was kind enough to us.

There was another sign on the bus that said *ALWAYS Wear a Seatbelt.* The man in the picture had no head and hands like a Simpson and we took no notice of his advice.

Some of the boys liked to goad other drivers, giving them the finger and the Vs and the wanker sign. Mooning from the backseats. It was like nothing they did on that bus would have any consequence. I didn't get involved, partly because I was afraid of getting in trouble and partly because I felt sorry for Coach. But I was on the bus, and therefore I was involved.

Josh Davies and a Dale twin picked a victim. A middle-aged Mondeo driver. Chubby, balding, glasses—a real three card trick. Davies blew kisses as Dale A or B pinched his thumb and pointer to make glasses of his own. The man tried to ignore them at first but was drawn into flashing a V.

"My brother's mate said that no-one sleeps in Ely," Wormy told us, oblivious to the man. "He said they just walk around all night."

I imagined a place of peeling paint and pellet guns. Sofas in the yard.

"Nah," Josh Davies said. "You gotta' sleep mun."

"You die if you don't sleep for like four days," Woody said.

"He's a copper, my brother's mate," Wormy continued. "He said he stopped a car in Glynneath once and found a bow and arrow."

"Hang on Worm, how's your brother running a pirating business if he's friends with policemen?"

"Policeman," Wormy corrected. "Singular. And Darren's sound as fuck."

Dale did the cock-in-your-mouth gesture. Davies licked his lips. Mondeo Man went ape.

"I heard they do so many drugs in Ely that the fish in the river started talking."

"How'd the drugs get in the river?"

"Flushing them down the toilet, innit?" Woody explained. "In your piss and that."

Mondeo Man sounded his horn, swerved in and out of traffic. If coach noticed he didn't say anything. Davies and Dale were pissing themselves laughing.

"Sully, does sewage go in the river?" Phillips shouted.

"I don't know," I said, watching Mondeo Man. "Ask Coach."

"Coach," Phillips called. "Coach?"

Mondeo Man had a face like an unripe strawberry. Like a popped balloon.

"Anyone know where the fuck we are?" Alien asked, boxing the seat in front of him.

"We passed a sign that welcomed us to Rhondda something something," I said. "Wherever that is?"

"Fuck," Alien said. "That's pretty close."

Alien put his name down for the army too, the only difference being he would actually end up in Afghanistan. He met Ross Kemp out there. Posted the picture on Facebook.

"What's the big deal about Ely?" Alex asked, eyes closed against Alien's pummelling.

"They're mad," Alien said. "Fucking nutters."

"What you reckon they think about us?" Alex asked. "Why d'you think

Porthcawl call us mountain men? The banjo pluckers?"

"Because they're posh cunts?" Alien tried.

The other thing Alien would put on Facebook was a suicide note. He said stuff about being sorry, not being able to go on etc. He said it was all shit. He said Afghanistan was shit and the ragheads were shit and George Bush was shit too, and that he'd seen his friends die out there before he saw a single fucking *Talibani*. That's what he wrote. Talibani. I was never sure if it was a typo or Army thing or what.

The post was deleted but the page is still up. Every year it tells me to wish him a happy birthday.

*

The only thing I got from putting my name on the form was a load of catalogues through the post. I flicked through them and tried to imagine what wars they were fighting in the photographs. Past wars and future wars. Wars as imagined in boardroom brainstorms. I wondered what type of war I'd most like to fight in. What type of war I'd like to avoid.

The army spots potential. One booklet told me. *Even if others don't.*

*

Mondeo Man had been following for like quarter of an hour now, weaving between lanes and leaning on his horn. His anger surpassed the moment, transcended it, as though Davies and Dale hadn't caused the rage but merely let it free. He screamed and swore with spittle flying from his mouth. He beat the steering wheel with his hands.

Oblivious, a few boys got to discussing why we called Wormy Wormy. We had no idea. Boycey said he ate a worm in nursery, just picked it straight up out of the grass

"We call Wormy Wormy because of his tiny little worm dick," Woody said.

"When were you looking at my dick?"

"Saw it in the Guinness World Records."

"I thought we called Wormy Wormy because if you cut him in half, two grow back."

"You're thinking of the Dale twins."

"It's like a game of *Where's Wally* in Wormy's pants," Woody said. "You need a fucking magnifying glass."

Mondeo Man was puce and screaming, eyes popping out of his head as he swerved across the lanes.

Perhaps there's a point of no return in anger. Once you commit, you're in, and never getting out again. Once you're that angry, you'll be angry all your life.

We all watched now, saying nothing beyond oh shit, oh shit. He sped up the outside lane, eyeing us in the windows and waving his fists. He pulled out across the front of the bus and fell back on the inside lane, gesturing all the while.

Maybe it's a matter of pride. A matter of logistics. There's simply no path back to normality when fury is unleashed.

The music had stopped, the only sound that of our breathing and the great rush of the road. The laughing had stopped too. I eyed Davies, his pale face, his fidgeting hands. He wanted to do something else, I realised.

Humiliate the man even more.

"Don't mun," I found myself saying. "Leave him."

Mondeo Man had fallen in behind us, right up our arse, and Davies got out of his seat. He stepped over the balls and boot bags, over Perry on the floor, and pressed his face to the back window.

"Oi, leave it," Woody warned. "Fucking sit down."

I saw Coach's eyes in the rear-view mirror.

Davies stared at the man and the man stared back. Each refused to blink. Alien got out of his seat to try and grab Davies but before he could reach him Davies tilted back his head. dragged a finger across his throat.

We looked at the man for a reaction and were surprised to see him fall back. What couldn't have been a metre between our bumpers was now five, then ten, his face shrinking into a blur.

Arms aloft like a victorious boxer, Davies turned to face his audience just as the Mondeo came hurtling back into focus. His car seemed bigger than before, filling the back window. For the strangest moment we sat in the pocket of time between being hit and feeling it, then Davies and Alien were flying over our heads.

Another thing Alien posted on Facebook was this video of an Afghan man, his head wrapped in black. The man was surrounded by other men, all facing the camera, He bellowed at the top of his lungs in Arabic. The clip was set to music, swelling electronics and ghostly whispers. A hand holding a BBC News microphone jutted into the bottom of the frame.

"We say to the Britishers it is not the Taliban who are fighting you," the man said, his words subtitled and furious. "If you don't know this, take a look at your history." The other men fiddled with the cloth on their faces. They nodded their heads and shifted weight from foot to foot. "It is the Afghan land which is fighting against you."

Soon the men were cheering, stamping their feet, raising fists in triumph. "See all these men?" the man continued. "They are Taliban. But they haven't come from abroad. They are Mujahideen who will take the Britishers out of our country."

The camera zoomed in and panned across the men. Across their Russian rifles and rocket-propelled grenades, their shemaghs white and black and pale blue. Eyes nervous and mean, united by circumstance and the words of their spokesman. Arabic was a beautiful language, a harsh language, a language of the tongue and throat.

"And if all the Afghans die," the man said, "the soil of Afghanistan will haunt you and destroy all of you."

*

By the time we picked ourselves up, the Mondeo Man had gone. Coach was shouting questions and we were shouting answers. I'm not sure who was the first to laugh but it was shaky and spontaneous. Coach didn't even pull over.

Soon we were all laughing, all yelling, joyous in the aftermath. We spoke about anything and everything, us boys. We challenged the world.

Amid the jubilation, I tried to see where we were. The Ely estate must have been close by then. But the windows of the bus had steamed up with all the shit we were talking.

Rachel Oliver, *What did you do to save the world today?*

Transatlantic, The Moon Flies with Me

By Margot Morgan

You reminded me a year ago that it was time for me to make a pilgrimage Stateside, that you knew it would replenish me as it always had. You were right. Since you've been gone, I must be near the sea.

I travel 'nor'-east, needing to retrace familiar ground. At Newport Beach the waves break red with seaweed, and I think of the Gododdin, the ancient blood and mead-soaked elegy that struck you, shaping your words; I think of how we talked over red wine of our distress at the violence abroad; I think of how we said how very lucky we were, how very rich we were.

A young girl wears a tee-shirt that says 'love'. The beach is full of baby gulls and I remember our last swim together, naked in the sea, autumn beckoning.

The splash of my feet in the shallows, sunlight shattering.

Further north the blue sky days roll one into another. At Boothbay Harbour I sail on a friendship sloop and feel the comfort of being with strangers. The seasoned captain tells how the seals are multiplying now that hunting them is illegal; there is talk of sharks foraging inland in search of them for food. But these waters are too cold for sharks she reassures, and later I swim without fear. The tide is low, a hurricane miles out at sea has landed a slippery bed of weed along the water's edge. Heavy red ribbons barnacled and torn, bladderwrack and tree-like shapes tangle my ankles. Hermit crabs and schools of tiny silver fish startle as I wade.

On the ride out to Louds Island the surf slaps the bow and the breeze threatens to deprive me of yet another favourite sunhat. Long dead Cecil the lobsterman who ferried our family here summers past, the sparkle of his eyes in the water. I always wished you could have known him. We shared such sea stories, you and I. Some years I'd come alone to stay with Cecil and his wife and be allowed out fishing. We'd leave the dock at sunrise, and I'd ride the prow of the boat or struggle to prove my metal and band the lobsters' claws. We round Little Harbour, and the smell pulls in my chest.

Ankle deep I bring the outboard ashore and thank the driver. The stink of gasoline hits as he gurgles gently out to sea and I want to throw myself on childhood's beach, but there is sea glass to gather, stone to reacquaint myself with and an islander or two to visit. I carry live lobster up to Mrs Marong who is too old this year, at eighty-seven, to bring her own boat out. I haven't seen her since my father died twenty years ago. The smell of her kitchen is comforting; gas lanterns, wild blueberries baking and fir trees through the back door. I promise to write. I hike the length of the island on one of two mud rutted roads seeking soldier moss, old man's beard, and solitude.

Wind soughs the pines, your grave a thousand miles away.

The fisherman who picks me up has been drinking. "The people change", he repeats, "The people change, but the island is always the same… It always stays the same."

At the Jersey Shore on the way home from the diner I'm surprised to find hundreds of families on the beach flying kites of all descriptions: floating boats, free of the water in the rose-edged evening. The sky darkens, huge waves driven by offshore storms thrash the shoreline seemingly in silence against the noise of children, their parents and the fluttering.

Back in suburbia Labour Day has friends and family scurrying, intent on being together and being somewhere special as summer fades. I have my mind on home across the more than three thousand miles that usually separate me from my mother, my siblings, their offspring, and my childhood friends. I spend the last days with mom—mum, doing what I can to make her as comfortable as possible before I leave her. She asks me again, "How long was he sick? Did you know that he was sick?" At ninety-four years, her face is beautiful.

Transatlantic. The moon flies with me.

Philippa Brown, *Sister Solidarity*

Luminous Bardess Earth to Sun Energies Awaken

By H Raven Rose

Hear!
    Birthed from Ceridwen's womb
    Dressed in Taliesin's star shine,
    That feminine animus sword of pen and poem,
    A journey to the home of our Celtic ancestors,
    Where a woman shaped the land,
    And women were its guardian,
    Mother Earth's protector and the bearer of wisdom,
    and the king married her land-body,
    walked by the People of the Raven,
    and the woman might forge a path to herself
    through the dark forest of her pain.
    Home to Wales, where one might heal the heart,
    Hold the grief-stricken Inner Child(ren),
    And help her learn to sing her song with the tongue of a swan,
    despite the evils of the world.
    Your soul parts are aligned,
    And in this reading, your soul aligns with mine.
    The Father Sun above us, the Mother Earth below.
    Flight to the light of the red-gold star,
    Rooted in the bogs and shadowy glades,
    the beaches, wells, and Wales, water with the spark of life,
    so hard to find these days.
    Divine union and a journey to the Self
    can only be made in the place of our ancient blood.
    Feel your body, feel your heart, feel your grief, touch your shining brow, beauty.
    Your awen, poetic flow, magic stardust liquid pen elixir
    follows the wild hunt for the blackest nigredo,
    That Stygian night of the soul,
    Which is found in the ffau, the ffeuau, the cave, the sacred enclosure, the
    earth vessel, by which we descend into our darkness, transcend the profane,

the anghofrwydd or forgetfulness,
To find purification of pain, the albedo of body, the shadow in the cauldron
of one's being.
'Allwyn. Allwyn. Allwyn', someone sibrwd from the gardd, the garden. 'Sad. Sad.
Sad',
the whisperer repeats in a singsong from another world.
'You're too sad', says the Tylwyth teg clothed in white, red, and green,
Who live by the hundred-year-old garden wall,
'You're hurting us', they say, gleaming eyes appalled by human grief.
So, offerings are made by the hedge. Songs of apology, organic local South Wales
honey, amber nectar, mint and flowers, the face of the goddess, and rose quartz
crystal for love.
Because one's grief is a morphogenic field of pain that touches everyone,
in every realm, even those shining gold silver glittering lustrous palatial places.
Then a focus on joy and gratitude and a hike down the Wales Coast trails,
Where by a field one may take a step and fall three feet down,
and into the gorse, the lemon-yellow lovelight, in the hidden ditch there,
and fall upward into the meddygaidd, the medicine, golden hope and the sage's
citrinitas future,
a mystical journey to travel between the human and spirit worlds.
Yet it is only on primaeval loam, the soil of one's people,
That this ancient alchemy may happen,
That these luminous bardess earth to sun energies awaken,
The frequencies which resonate upward from the mother earth,
And awaken the ancient DNA and cells within a grounded body and being.
The energies resonate downward from the Father Sun.
Each day the woman be remade in this the truer life.
Each day a woman be a lightning rod for the luminous splendour of spirit, and
awen crowns her,
The rubedo sun star drips the liquid gold of her purpose, words and truth
through her body and being and into her hands and feet.
Feet that walk the profane level of culture, with its evil and decay,
Feet that trod the road of the split soul reunited, life and breath,
In a land where mist slips down the side of a mountain,
Where a star we've once seen is an opening, doorway, to the luminaries,

A land where any hour might blot all pain away,
One's heart metronome might beat transcendence,
through a soul door to the world above.
Each day a woman holds the Inner Child(ren) until their tears dissipate like the
mist and rain burnt away by rays of golden summer sunlight on the sea-brine
kissed shores of the Gower.
'Bardess', breathe-sing the emerald flocked trees in Swansea when we bless and
heal them, 'A bardess in Wales', they sing with their tree-voice hum-song breath
tinged with wonder.
Ground into your body and receive the blessed, ancient medicine of our soul song.
Each day be a vessel between our mother Earth of Cymru and our Father Sun above.
Soul songs from a distant star ground into Cymru, ground into you.
And these are the secrets whispered by the forests and the most ancient yw, the
Yew trees, the ywydd, in Laugharne undimmed by light pollution, where the man-
boy bard lies sleeping still.
And these are the mysteries Rhiannon's birds will murmur in your shell-shaped ear.
Eryi, Snowdonia, holds up the world and calls us to spiral upward, to arch and bow
from illusion to the enchanted.
At Cadair Idris, we sleep away our manmade madness and awaken.
And in Pentre Ifan, we find the mysteries and enter the portal fashioned from
Pembrokeshire bluestone.
And then in Annwvn, the Otherworld, we might drink from the pool of luscious
language,
Despite the battered, bruised, beaten, abused body that lives in the wasteland of
the world,
Because in the Annwvn the women hold the cup, the wisdom, and we drink
deeply of the Awen,
Breathing in the scent of fae fishes of silver and gold.
The stardust of liminal liquid inspiration golden elixir remains on our lips when
we of the Buddug bodice return to this middle world.
Hear! There is ancient healing enchantment—iachâd rhinweddol—for women
afoot on the earth. Woman with red dragon blood ready to ripen, eager to die to
the past and fly on wings of ravens to the Otherworld, might heal her wound,
her anaf. That living goddess might recreate her narrative and find her owl-faced
flower heart and pure, white Blodwyn soul in Wales.
Here is a feather. Here is a flower. Here is your pen. Find your way home, bardess.

Arron Kuiper, *It's Getting on for One*

Some kind o beginnin

By Mike Jenkins

The sound o voices rises from-a street. More banterin 'an arguin, but it still brings back tha night. There's too many thin's remind me. Ev'ry time I see Dave on telly playin f'r the Jacks. Ev'ry time I go out to a Club (though tha int often nowadays) an there's a barney.

Puttin on my face, layer 'pon layer, I carn elp thinkin ow she must afto dollop it on t cover over wha I done. An there by-a mirror is-a cuttin. People might think I'm sick or summin, but I jest don' wanna forget. It's a warnin: never agen!

Wish I woz goin out with them girlz. Theyer jokin pierces-a glass an ruffles-a curtains. A whool gang of em I bet, like we woz in Merthyr: me, Nadine, Andrea an Jayne (with a 'y' don' forget, she'd always say). I long f theyer voices now goin up an down like-a mountains an valleys.

Funny tha, it's flatter down by yer, but the way they talk ave got the same mewsic to it.

Mascara, face cream … owever much I put on, I could never be like er. My teeth stick out in a funny way an I got ooded eye-lids like my dad wuz an owl or summin. I light up a fag an burn an ole jest above er ead. I 'member wha ee once said, 'Martine, I'm sorry t tell yew, but yewer breaths mingin … yew should try an give up.' But all them months in the Centre I needed em so much. I could never give up now, not even if I seen im agen.

The thin's the papers said, an mostly true I know. But oo cun understand all tha goadin? All tha gangin up an pickin on me er frens done? It woz like Cardiff against the Jacks, we all knew it wuz gunna kick off some time, but no-one spected me t make it appen.

I blow smoke at er picture. The eadlines blur. I yer my flat-mate Chrissie come ome from work: tide job in-a Travel Agents, all dolled up. She's like me, tryin t make a new life. She've ad 'n ard time, brought up in-a Omes. Carn understand ow she's so down-t-earth an kind though. TV on, cuppa tea nex …

'Hey Martine! D' you wanna cuppa?'

'No ta, Chrissie! I'm off soon!'

She knows all 'bout me, but it don' bother er. She reckons er dad done worse thin's to er an er mam.

Tha bloody burn above er air looks like a friggin alo! I feel like turnin tha photo t ash once an f'r all, but instead I stub-a fag out on-a mirror, right where my teeth jut out comical.

Chrissie looks so relaxed in-a sittin room when I enter, feet up an sippin away. As she turns er ead, f'r a second she reminds me of er, tha beaky nose an pointy chin, but then …

'Martine, you look great!' she says, an I do feel ready
t face the world, even though I wan more.

'Aye, but oo cares in tha poncy otel?'

'Well, maybe you'll meet someone tonight. Some millionaire soccer star'll be passing through and propose to you over his lasagne!'

'Soccer star?'

'Oh . . . sorry Martine!'

I larf an she wriggles in er chair an echoes me. Soon it's 'S'long!' and 'Bye!' Me wonderin ow she cun talk so posh with er background an ave survived.

The streets o Abernedd turnin inta Merthyr by the second. Cack-jumpin an spottin where yesterday's shops ewsed t be. See-through windows replaced by an environmentally-friendly sort, perfect f'r graffiti an posterin. Local bands like Panic Stations an The Pocket Billiards advertisin gigs. I woz inta football when my friends listened t the Merthyr equivalents o them. I woz turned on when Merthyr played the Jacks (Dave wern with em 'en) an stood with Dazzy an the boys chantin an loathin to a pitch where I lost myself.

Wassa time? Shit! Four minutes late an moany ol cow Thorpe'll be bound t dock me.

Car beeps me. Two boys in overalls, all over painty. Give em a V and see em mouthin off at me.

There it is at bloody last, The Dog and Duck, Abernedd's finest, 3 star, AA. Looks real tidy from-a front an all, but I could blow it open, wha with ol Thorpey an is stingy ways . . . scrapin-a mould off of fruit an tha ol can-opener sheddin rust!

'Yer! Wha's this in my peas, waitress?'

'Oh, I believe it's some sort o garnish, sir.'

When in doubt, call it garnish, tha's wha ee tol us t say.

Just as I'm gaspin f'r a fag an fumblin in my pockets, Thorpey ops through-a door t greet me.

'Martine, you're five minutes late again. It'll have to stop, Marteen!'

Sayin my name like I woz 'n alien. Feel sorry f'r is missis, I do. Imagine im on top on the job . . . 'You've had your ten seconds heavy-petting, dear. Now we'd better hurry up and start breathing faster!'

'Marteen! Stop grinning and get ready, will you!'

Soon I'm all frilled up an layin-a tables, all-a time chattin t Michelle oo on'y jes started las week an oo keeps cockin ev'rythin up. She's so nervous an tryin t please, but Thorpey give er so much jip when she wrote-a orders down wrong, she nearly give up on er first day. An the bloke what ad steak 'n' kidney pie 'stead o steak! I thought ee wuz gonna crack er one on-a spot!

Lee, the main chef, ee takes-a piss outa Mich no end. Ee tried it with me when I begun, so I tol Mich t take no notice. But she don' know when ee's bullin or not. Ee tol er the correct way t serve chips wuz with a fork an she believed im. By-a time she'd got em on-a plate, they'd frozen agen!

Friday evenin, but it's real quiet. I serve a family with a stroppy veggie wife an two kids insistin on avin adult portions.

'What's this Vegetable Steak Casserole?' she asks.

'Oh no,' I says, 'tha's vegetable casserole with steak in it.'

'But it does say Vegetable Steak, doesn't it?'

This coulda gone on forever, on'y er ol man tells er t ave-a veggie lasagne.

Lee's outa is ead as per usual. I reckon ee's on summin, I do.

'One veggie lasagne, but I reckon there's some rat in it somewhere, Martine . . . Look! There's its brother!' ee yells, pointin is spatula at-a corner of-a kitchen. I twirl round like a ballerina, then give im a shove in is bulbous beer-gut an ee makes out t swat me like a fly. Mich comes in lookin all excited like she seen some lush pop-star. She catches old o my arm, while I'm on-a look-out f'r ol Thorpey, oo always seems t rush in when we int workin tidy.

'Martine! There's these really ace boys! . . . Yew gotta come an give me an and! I'm on pins!'

'Aye, I will, arfta I done this one table. Okay?'

So I takes in the veggie lasagne an the usband's ome-made pie (what comes straight from-a freezer) an ave a gawk. There's a loada tables put together an, jest as Mich said, a pile o stonkin men and boys in posh suits an flash ties. Then I see Thorpey chattin to 'n older man oo wuz with em an ee glares over at me, so I make out I'm busy servin the famlee.

As I'm dishin out-a veg, I yer a Merthyr voice an 'n unmistakable one at tha. I practically fling-a veg onto the bloke's lap an spatter im with gravy.

The back end o Dave's ead, I'm shewer.

'Excuse me!' says the bloke.

'Oh, I'm sorry!' I grovel, in case ee should call Thorpey. I do a rapid runner back to-a kitchen an grab old o Mich, oo's gotta andfull o prawn cocktails.

'Well, Martine, what d'yew think, eh?'

'Mich! Lissen! There's this boy I ewsed t know there . . . I think theyr Swonzee football team . . . I gotta do the next servin, right?'

Coz I'm so igh-pitched an wound up, Lee yers me over is sizzlin chip-oil an steak-bashin. Is face is a pumpkin grin.

'Ne' mind the rat, where's the fuckin poison? I could never stick the Jacks!'

'Don' be darft, Lee. Ee's from Merthyr.'

'Ey, Mart, I thought yew woz a true Bluebird.'

'Tha's all in-a past . . . Right, Mich, give us them prawn cocks!'

Michelle's nearly creamin er knicks on-a spot, she's so worked up.

'Ey, we could be on yer . . . I fancy the big black one, I do!'

'I gotta black puddin in the fridge, if yew don't get off with im,' shouts Lee.

'Shurrup Lee, y' racist dick!' I yell as Mr Thorpe comes bustin through-a door. Ee's tampin an is ard white face its me like a breeze-block.

'Martine,' ee whispers snakey, 'just get on with the job or you're out! Right?'

I feel like tellin im t stuff it, but I iss back 'Yess, Mr Thorpe!' I go calm but quick inta the dinin area an make a point o servin Dave first. I glance over t see Mich urryin towards the big black fella, oo looks real chuffed. Dave's busy talkin, so I lean right over im, cranin t face im like I wuz goin t give im a peck.

'Yewr prawn cocktail sir!' I says, so deliberate an sarky ee turns straight away, lookin curious till ee recognises me. Is eyes 'n mouth narrow inta three blades. Then ee turns away with a flick of is ead like ee wuz eadin-a ball or summin.

As I return to-a kitchens I yer im callin me back. I don' wanna respond, but thinkin o Thorpey's warnin, I decide to.

'Uh . . . scuse me, waitress, but can I ave my steak well done, please? I carn stand the sight o blood!'

An all-a players larf, like it woz some private joke.

'Yes, of course sir!' I feel like spittin out-a words, but I control myself, savin it up. Inside, I'm so angry coz ee treated me like I woz nobuddy. All is indifference brings it back: ow ee ewsed me against er, er against me. I seen ow ee wanted us t be total enemies. An I played is game orright . . . a Stanley knife I on'y brung f'r protection . . . she wuz avin a go at me all-a time . . . 'Martine, yew've lost im, yew bitch! Le's face it, yewr a loser!' . . . Blood everywhere. Now I gotta remember. Er blood on my clothes an ands: I knew I'd never wash off them stains. An when Dave says 'bout is steak jest then it seemed aimed, like is sharp eyes shinin.

I decide t take in these special steak knives we aven ewsed frages an Lee thinks I'm darft.

'Wha yew wanna bother with them for? I need em f choppin up the rats anyway.'

'Lee do me favour an chop yewrself up, they'll be one less rat then.'

I rub my and cross-a blade o one. I feel scared an thrilled at-a same time. Mich comes in grinnin all over er body, as if she've orreadly got tha fella. I old up-a knife towards er.

'Ey, Martine! Go easy! I never spoke to yewers. Onest!'

'It's okay, Mich. This one's f'r im!' I clatter-a knives onto a tray, leavin Michelle stunned.

This time I take it real slow, as if I woz strokin. I know wha I'm doin, so I ask oo's avin steak an watch is face as I carefully place each knife. I old each one a while before puttin it down an I cun see is panic risin. Ee cun see I'm leavin im till last an ow much I'm relishin it all. Looks as if ee's shittin is load when I finally come t im.

'Yew avin steak, sir . . . Well done, wern it?'

'Er . . . aye . . . ta!' ee tries t act so cool, but is ands 're fiddlin with is other cutlery, as if ee's searchin f weapons!'

I take old o the las steak-knife an prepare t show im. Now ee'll get the message. I cun take down tha cuttin. I cun wash off tha red. I sweep the knife up to is face an ee jerks back in is chair, nearly fallin. At-a same time, Michelle comes in screamin, 'Don' do it, Martine! Don' do it agen!'

An I says t Dave, real calm . . . 'Is this done enough f'r yew sir?'

Ev'rythin appens so quick, I think I've sliced im without knowin. Is team-mates 're laughin, Michelle grabs my arm an Thorpey's fussin an pullin me back t the kitchen. Ee drags me outa the door inta the yard. I still gotta knife, but there's no blood anywhere t be seen.

'This is no joke, Martine! How dare you treat our customers like this? Who do you think you are? You can't . . .'

I fling the knife to the ground an-a sound severs is words, leaves em angin.

'Yew cun stick yewer bloody job, Mr Thorpe! I wozn messin, f yewr information, it wuz f'r real. I owed tha boy one!'

'I should never have taken you on . . . I knew about your record, you know . . . They told me you'd changed
. . . Now, get out of my hotel!'

I undo-a apron an scrumple it up as ee shoves past me. I fling it in-a bin an feel a real buzz, though ee never seen me.

As I stride away down-a street, a coach passes an faces stare at me with a 'Wow!' on theyer lips. All of em 'cept one, that is. I lost so much to im: my body, my freedom an now my job. I'll go ome an take-a scissors to er photo. Cut it up inta tiny pieces knowin tha won' be the end, but tha problee this is some kind o beginnin.

Previously published in *Barkin'* published (Carreg Gwalch), *Child of Dust* (Gomer) and *Stories from Wales* (Parthian).

Being Culted
a true story

By Samantha Mansi

Arron Kuiper, *Down in the Valley*

As if being culted was not bad enough, losing my belongings ... going up and down on trains from South Wales to the Scottish borders. It sounds like a movie? It's true life. It's why I began my Masters in Creative Writing and it's why I want to become a writer. Struggling with PTSD after being culted was hard enough, without the authorities just totally deserting me. Sure, they helped me with the court process but that was about it.

So, what is it like to be coerced out of two different refuges? It's absolute hell, when you feel totally unsafe. You believe someone with mental health issues that you are coerced back to him and to more trauma. As much as it's a blur, I do remember the kindness of people and despite the fact I thought I was losing my mind I have got out and I'm able to tell the tale.

Being culted in an end of the world cult it's frightening. I stopped watching the TV and the news really triggered me as well. He would say—

my abuser—*Look they are bringing in the microchip* and all sorts of bizarre things. He believed in things such as clone factories and flat earth theories. My breakdown was caused by my work in the Yorkshire ambulance service, and I got taken off emergency calls due to some errors. I felt like a total failure and was upset. However, my ex had seemed like a way out—to what was going on. We had intimacy and he said I was his wife, that God had put us together. It sounds strange to believe that—but when your headspace isn't great it's easy to become vulnerable to such predators. The story goes on and on with many twists and tales. But unfortunately, the British system does not allow much space for cult survivors. Nor is there much support given. Luckily, I worked on self-care, and found I like writing poetry and spending time with animals. I like time walking and in nature as well. So, whatever you're going through you will get there and don't give up—please reach out for help.

Arron Kuiper, *Through Fathers who Left No Bones*

Outside the World

By Karl Francis

The world outside is ready for bed. A single swallow on the line singing out the season.

Time is late this year.

Autumn is just round the corner, mark my word.

I don't know somewhere along the way we've gone and lost the seasons.

Outside, a pitman with a poodle for company the cold clear night time air telling tales of long ago when men were men when boys would be boys remember Dai Penn home from America next week, go on, now he threw the brick that put the policeman's eye out the day they read the riot act where the coop used to be never should have been here anyway Liverpool policemen laying down the law to common working men the day after the Lockout. I never went back for seven years until the war came, they wanted me then when the bombs were there digging holes into their profits, and me a pacifist in the first war that's when I took up dogs always the same dogs except this one, belongs to the missus won it in a raffle the Sisterhood sweep, you get used to them mind women as well. History outside a window passing the time of night with a woodbine and bingo the poodle peeing a line up the lamppost for women to say dirty bugger in the morning, passing the time before the elderberry wine got the spit up to keep winter at arm's length a little bit longer, just another collier with a cough he looked after a bit better.

Old men walking and listening and talking and waiting for their dogs to catch up and do the same thing and then to carry on.

Who's living there now gone to bed early up to no good I bet the best of British luck I say? Footsteps silent as the night good night god bless good night god bless. Silent night.

And along the street Mrs Watsit's twins tucked tightly in warm and snug in their single divan playing cheerfully with their identical things seeing nothing but their dreams under the blankets as their mother sat down below to a second helping of the dream machine waiting for Albert to come home hot and sweaty and stinking with beer from the afternoon shift ready to cool her off outside the world.

As an observer what do you think of the human race Albert Evans? Hush now you'll keep the street awake.

Temper, temper.

Leave the box on nice and loud that's loud enough that way they'll never the hear the noise.

Showing off again the one twin said fast asleep which one I couldn't tell.

She saw none of this, she lay half asleep the pink papered room paying homage to the neon lights of the growing town but soon she would be gone again home to another nest like the early morning sparrow on the line outside.

I'm on my own too, the four-square wall and window night and day hiding her nakedness from the outside world. A leaf always falls ... sooner or later. But for her autumn never the same, only a woman growing old, a body growing cold, a woman in winter.

You're only a child memory said.

I'm older than you'll ever be.

The swallow is an early morning bird, why sit you now tonight. Like you I got my dates wrong love.

This way I get a worm's eye view of the Welsh upside down again. Mad, just talking love only words they can't harm anyone.

As for the man whose body lay next to her and in whose bed she lay, her breasts had been to him as white and soft as Ponti's ice cream, two cornets playing their tune on a Sunday afternoon curled up in the ferns softening the lips cooling the brain, gone soft with love's ambition with grass snakes and adders and horsefly and the wind before the babies came for company. I am a breasts man boy lipsticked to her bum.

The words spun their web as gracefully then as they did now. He was not a man to question anything he said words lie buried in the past the birth of something new thoughts growing up like leaves on trees always the same, always different, until they are expressed and then are lost and are never really caught in books until tomorrow when it will have grown into something else the chemistry in our veins the smell of stale furniture a newspaper line. But believe in it, it is your thought. It belongs to you.

A window on a starlit night, shadows of a distant smile, turn over now just talking love, I see myself, two eyes two ears a hand a nose a thought an image trying to compose a question to the gods it saw no more distant now seeing nothing I claim eternity and on believing all there is what else is there to see.

Blind is the sea in the eye of the fish, deaf is the wind to the buzz of a bee, trees full of honey suckle a smile for the tramp fast asleep in the world out of doors. Only a thought not to be believed.

She lay as she was born to lie the way her mother taught her in the womb the open window watching her shouting out her nakedness twice as loud for none to see. She lay the sweet stale taste of love. Love still in her lips. Her fingers gently walking in their sleep, milking a dead future from within his loins. The battle for tomorrow's world begins.

The armies of the early night show little life but dawn is breaking now. He's up before you again this morning she whispered kissing the gift of sight upon his eyes, you're not even a challenge she smiled I like it like that, living in the present all the time never on Thursday this or that never harking back, only a thought gone now but coming back to be taken seriously in the second half those words born to ring dry the minutes after sleep the dew without a dawn to ride upon, the world and me as clear as washing dishes.

Voices speak, talk to me now sing me a story of Jack and the Glory ... tell me a tale of ducks and drakes and birds and bees and alligators snakes dressed up in the emperor's clothes and little things all in a row. 'It belongs to me this thought,' she thought, 'clutch it to your angry.' 'Should' he said, believe it's mine. The madness grows it too belongs to me and in my sleep I knew nothing of it.

Only my past belongs to me. I have nothing else.

What else is there to be. Seek I the flower or the thorn. My thoughts belong to me.

Is that all I have. Are we no more than the words which separate us? How easily your words conquered my imagination making me laugh, making me smile, making me think, believe in me I am a hurricane a blind virgin tapping out the time on Paddington Station, the memory began, it belongs, to me he said.

There is a time between dreams and life when sleep and fantasy mix with reality providing hope and love for the future. There is nothing unusual in that. And when the past with all its hate and wasted years of womanhood looking for love around the corner of some other girl's street, young thoughts losing their virginity to good looking madmen chasing the truth with all the blunt cruel force of an animal wanting something because someone else already has it, convinced that you are experienced because you look like that, don't give me that I know you are, and wanting it because of that, the past meant nothing then, they said I was thick at school, I never forgot I never was, my thoughts are as good as yours my tired scrubbers thoughts, within my brain is experience without intelligence but how my past seems to grow when the possibility of a future begins to exist.

But she didn't say that, instead she said what she had become accustomed to say and said nothing. Intelligence is nothing more than words the college boy had said and they're easy to come by. And she remembered these words when she remembered nothing else, people talk to build and the idea grows as others contribute like a river becomes dangerous in a flood, and I am right otherwise my entire life has been a useless waste of time, I am right because my scrubbers experience is now yours, my life already contains yours and it is me you are writing about.

And she thought how wise he was with his weakness deeply hid with strength in his body, but she didn't say that. Thoughts through a window a thirty-year-old smile with a little love left to spare time on my hands. Thirty years old today left-over love to love two birthday cards and a smile time out after ten with children asleep who'd be a woman by choice, you wouldn't believe me love, easy now, a scrubber without a lover, a girl on the loose, don't be afraid *why me* she thought.

But how easy it had been to make love to a man whose name she didn't know mad as a hatter in the Godiva Club you wouldn't believe me love. Honest. Awake at last. Never again I don't think.

Voices through a window sounds that only the lips may hear and understand softly now all round the house. And me a scrubber looking out, only a girl once, nothing to say in the Secondary School, and then a bread girl with two half-baked bastards in the oven to keep it warm he said, nice and warm, and then he'd gone away to sea trusting the silence to keep my tongue not so long ago.

Arron Kuiper, *Of Water Course*

Bootings

By Maj Ikle

I wave, but Alice doesn't wave back. We have lived together for years, shared meals, sat in morning meditation for a what feels like a decade, so her not waving back now, means we must both walk past one another in an ear breaking; mind messing; blood rushing silence of knowing we aren't going to be friends again today.

Unable to bear to watch her look through me, like I am empty of meaning, less than an obstacle, I lower my eyes to the ground. My eyes watch her boots come level with mine. My eyes observe how both sets of boots are, far more similar than they are different. Both sets encrusted with mud, both fiercely functional, waterproof, nut kicker style boots. Boots that say, 'We don't care what people think about our footwear, what people think women like us are like', our boots, come side by side now like family members, sharing paths as well as treads, treads as well as traits, traits which are busy with metaphoring how strong we show ourselves to the outside world.

How deliberately innocent we are of that world's expectations. How coherently we choose to ignore those ridiculous, dangerous expectations; how ignoring them is our sign to each other how capable we are to choose for ourselves good footwear, safe, strong, easy to run in shoes that will take us as far as we need to go. Far and away from the people who demean and demand from us, to any desires of us to be nice girls. These not nice girl shoes stride us through fields, clamber with us over ditches and beyond sexism, beyond patriarchy to here. Here and these valleys of our remote location, our separate space, out of their way, out of harm's way in a place to repair our wounds, our tiny piece of land where we can rest, rest and find our feet again.

Our feet that have walked us so far away from the traps and prisons kept ready for us, feet armored in shoes, in strong, solid, reliable walking kit that we proudly bought and paid for by ourselves. So proud that somehow, we have out-prouded one another, used our boots to keep on walking, keep walking even now away from one another.

Alice has turned to see me as different from her, different to how I once was to her. I have fallen short of her expectations in some irreconcilable way, fallen foul of her invisible trip wire, the trip wire that she uses to keep the boring and bad people away, she has found me guilty of being the 'other' that she needs to separate herself from, that category of person no longer entitled to her friendly wave or company.

Alice's boots disappear out of my line of sight, boots once used to walk towards one another as home, now stomp away, leaving me to hold tightly silent to my thumping heart. Trying hard to stop the gut wrenching of distress that these petty close encounters bring to stay brave even in the face of these daily ignorings. I try not to feel it, try to pull myself together by some handy bootstraps to remain a militant believer in Alice's freedom to walk on by, even in the face of how hard it is for me to bear the loss. The heart-breaking loss of smiles and waves and looks, from the lips and hands and eyes of a long loved, now greatly missed, even when she is only a few feet away, good friend.

Thirteen

By Alys Einion

Why am I telling this story? Because it is the root of the mountain that is my life now, the heart and hearth of it all, where the first flames of who I would become were kindled, and a light was lit in me that never really went out.

These were strange times and strange waves of knowing, body growing, breathing life into a being that would become me, someone I saw inside out as me expanding, rounding, fleshing myself, woman-becoming, a nature story of seeds and growth and spring, this was my spring, my springing up and growing out and coming out, too, in the end. A mind forged by words and fertilised by fantasy, their word not mine; I was the creation of every story I read, every dream I dreamed, my mind as fertile as warm wet earth, my body as wet and warm and lush as my mind, and the two connected in a sudden sexuality. We had moved, as a family, from the stigma-laden, watchful eyes of the council estate to a country pile, an old house with a history bleeding from its damp and crumbling walls. Ghosts roamed the corridors at night, breathing dreams of restless souls and women the lifeblood of home and hearth and family, and I was still learning this, still starting to see, still waiting for something more.

My mother spilled her bitterness into the world around her, and seasoned it with what she called love. My father was more present, yet less so, and I felt painfully the awkwardness of my emerging sexuality; in his proximity, I saw myself through his eyes, my first experience of the male gaze and the vulnerability of my visible womanhood. My sister, the nearest one, my almost-twin, eased through the world comfortably, secure in her acceptance; her rejection of me mirrored that of her friends and most of my peers. She disdained me; my exposed emotions, my passions, the dreams that persisted in transforming my nights into lived days and years; frequently I woke screaming and gasping, or crying; once I woke with a feeling of grief so complete, so profound, that I could scarcely move through that day or those that came after; there were no details, simply a blackness, and the grief, so real, seemed impossible to survive. My sister complained frequently about sharing a room with me, and it was her pressure on my parents that forced them to give me my own room, the year I turned thirteen. It was always so; whatever I asked for was denied, or postponed, but they would move mountains to please her, to keep her happy. She was slim enough to wear the clothes from the most fashionable shops; a size sixteen, I could not dress as stylishly nor carry off the outfits I longed to wear, and her glee at being better than me at this part of life—better at being a teenager, better at being a woman, better at being accepted, was a measure of her lifelong resentment of my intellect and aptitude, my detailed memory and the ease with which I negotiated the scholastic aspects of life.

My unconditional heart rejoiced; my sister sickened in the oozing damp rooms, but there was a coal fire in our bedroom, and the thin windowpanes framed a valley fronted in green and gold. Such riches, waves and seas of grass and fern and trees and wild, a mountainside long-ago tamed but speaking of so much freedom. She walked beside me, the sister so close she could be my twin, but she was the loved one, the thin one, the pretty one, and I, short and rounded and difficult, roamed rabbit-paths and sheep tracks and inward into mind-spaces where I tasted a new freedom, a freedom to be something other than the stories they used to tell me how to be.

A world pressing, mother looming large and ruling over an ancient kitchen range, juxtaposed with an electric cooker, giving forth her edicts and wisdom; a stranger, yet not, for as it always had been, the love was mixed with pain, with threat, with the threat of being seen, always watched, always scrutinised, even as my older twin ran wild and unnoticed, boys, eating disorders, disobedience. I, I was the difficult one, and there were no listeners to the deep dreams and wild mind turns of my life, and no witness to the tears that came with the rush of hormones new to me, new body, the same me, but writ large in a story of power.

This is what they taught me: everything is conditional. Love, food, home, family. Sex and Death. Your place in the world. Everything is a conditional clause, bound to the one before, and the one before that, and the one before that, all the way back to the first words and the first woman who felt, without words, the simple fatality of cause and effect. It was a power once, I read this in my very bones, in the chain of linked elements relating me to all women, to the first woman. I knew in myself a secret power, a lunar strength, waxing and waning, an earth strength, growing and holding, a fire that flamed and smouldered, but never went out. Around me were the strong women of family and community, in their overalls and hairnets and their going-out dresses. Beside me was the family that saw without knowing how that there was something wrong, something different, something beyond control, no matter how they tried.

There are stories of suffering in that deep earth, tales I was not told but which entered my dreams and coloured the tone of the world around me. Miners' strikes and families' suffering, but we were on the outside too, a part of but apart from the community drawing together. I roamed the old house and its shadows, and deep in the books that gave me grace and vision, I named the feelings and seeings, the new way of knowing, that told me of the woman I would be, could be, should be, then and now, that woman to be, becoming, coming out under that wide sky, high sky, a wider horizon than that seen from lower in the valley, but always that hilltop, calling me on, telling me there were stories to be seen and known and to live through, stories in which I was hero, not villain. Stories in which I was loved, just as I am. I wish you could see it, the way the sky changed from pale silver to white to grey of a morning, from a washed out chalk to steel and slate when the storms came in, from gold to blue to gold again on fine autumn days, but for me, it was forever spring, forever poised on the edge of fullness, waiting to be all I that I knew I could be.

The stories they told of me, to me, were full nots, and knots, twists and turns and interruptions to the pure, sweet, silver flow that I knew existed underneath it all—the life of spirit, soul, unassailable and unchanging. The life they painted for me in negative, everything I was not, everything I would never be, was a tale of their own creation, rooted in the disappointment of lives spent and years wasted and shamed, the same story told again in a different body. But at night, my dreams were all desire, fire and fullness and a new arousal, a never-named power of woman. How could I not have been told of this?

What can I tell you of that time? How can I evoke for you, the smells of stale cabbage, boiled grey, the rich smell of roasting meat, the sharp sour scent of the wine in its crocks, waiting for the demijohn? The smell of woodsmoke and sulphurous coal, dust and dirt and damp, of earth and the thin smell of splitting wood. The cold air, clean, the long shadows of the sun, the rambling hedge and tenacious grass between the ancient flagstones. Fir woods and wild rose, turned earth and the dank, dark death-smell of the old cellars with their green-painted doors, so low even I had to stoop to enter, and the earthen bricked walls, reddish brown and layered, and that one, horrible cellar. Two doors, three cellars, the central room bricked up, but the bricks were removed to allow us to see in. There is a horror story there; the gnarled and wizened tree root left in the secret cavern, the abode of great spiders that migrated upwards towards the warmth of the bedrooms above, sliding between the cracks in the floorboards to appear and wait for me or my sister to notice their monstrous limbs. Our fanciful imaginations were fired, but there was more, so much more, the awareness of layered histories and mysteries, of a world beyond this one, beyond the reach of language and memory, something written in the very earth itself

My mother was strong, powerful, wide-bodied and fleshed, capable, with a bright mind and quick understanding, but my father was none of these things, and so she hid, as did countless women, and dissembled, and became for him the weak woman he needed, and she joined him in hating her body and its beauty, its fleshly power written in the very folds and lines of belly and legs and thick, strong arms, the soft breasts that gave comfort to four children, the deep womb that gave us life. This was not what he wanted. His story, repeated so much it became a refrain, was of the slender woman he married, with the 23 inch waist; at times, rare times, the wedding dress would be brought out, yellowed now with age, the satin with its silk embroidery stained but still beautiful, a faded photograph of once upon a time, and we would wonder at it, my sisters and I, at the slenderness of the waist and arms, the fragility of this tiny garment, and we would see then the ghost of the woman my mother had been then, diminished, in our eyes, less than the greatness we knew now.

In a life measured by what you are not, there is never satisfaction, no sense that you are enough. Childhood punctuated by poverty, I knew about not-enough. Hunger and denial, the excitement of Christmas and birthdays when any gift was a real treasure, even cheap plastic and flimsy card, even a single book. But in the times of plenty, as they were then, at thirteen, there was a different kind of want. The world had a vision of fragile femininity, small and slender, easily bent and broken, easily controlled, and I was found wanting. I was formed from the bones and stones and earth of my land, and grew wild on stories of my mother's becoming, and wilder still on stories of my own, feeding myself with the promise of future freedom, and walking the thin line of fear and loss that must come with its realisation. Ostracised and punished in school for what would now be given a diagnosis, I relied on myself for company, and wept, sometimes daily, at the emptiness of a world bereft of love. I knew, in the words cast my way that year, that I was not worthy of it.

Blood came, a morning of expectation—deep down I knew that it was coming, this outward signifier of an inward transition—and I stumbled from the little lean-to toilet, through the draughty cold of the scullery with its butler sink and sagging wood shelves, the flagstone floor and the washing machine and freezer at drunken angles against the peeling paint of the wooden walls, and there was my mother, as always, in the kitchen, with the scent of coal and wood burning, the dry heat and food cooking, light from the north making stark the dirt and dust on the countertops and the yellow-pine table. I did not want to tell her, but I needed to. I waited for the wisdom, the kindness, the woman-to-woman moment, this, the time of accession to this version of me that I would live for the rest of my life. She spoke, when I confessed what had happened. She spoke words of disappointment; disgust in her tone, and no love, a twisted expression, dark with disgust. *Great, now you can get pregnant*. I was sent off to find my sister to borrow some necessary items, and nothing more was spoken of it, and I wept, flooded with shame and fear and loss, that this great, shining moment was lost in her story of my future. In the inevitability of it.

I was in the scullery again, weeks later, caught between one task and another, perhaps returning from chopping wood at the woodshed, when my older sister caught me, blonde hair perfect in a shaggy perm, taller than me, an adult, married and legitimised and accepted. She asked me about my friendship with a girl from school who had come for a sleepover that weekend. "You're not going to be one of them" she told me. She did not need to say more. We knew each other's meaning. She too had taken on the story-shape of the family, of telling me what I would not be, could not be, should not be. A few days later, my mother hissed the same warning at me, from her rooted position in the kitchen, wooden spoon in hand.

You will never, the same song sung at every family gathering or after every school report, standing on the carpet in the cavernous lounge, or perched on the edge of the new grey sofa, my mother in her knee-length skirt showing the folds and striations of her thick thighs through parted knees, my father standing; as a short man he stood when we sat, chest puffed out, drawing himself up to fill the space with his authority. You will never get married, you're too fat. You will never have children, never get to university, never get a decent job, never be anything. Hurt and pain, fleeing down the dark corridors to my room with its spiders and bookcase and a door that shut, and it was a kindness, really, they told me, a kindness because the world would treat me as they did, with the same rejection and disdain. This was the story they told me, the story of my worth, for my own good.

Then there was the story I told myself, of secret dark places and deep, dark scents of womanhood, of the softness and the firmness, the rising tide of sensation and the earth-shattering, body-reclaiming wonder of release, of the fullness and the fire, desire and delight. I learned my own pleasure one pale, sunset evening on a rush of music, a chair against the door, and in that I knew freedom, and myself, as a woman, as a human, as a whole entity, and it was all I needed to know, that this fleshly body, just a little too large, just a little too short, just a little too wide and strong, was my own to love, and like the earth it was born from, the stardust and cloudbursts and wide, waiting sky, it was my vehicle to glory and to greatness, to being and seeing beyond the narrow hills, outside the margins of the familiar stories, an aeon of creation written loud and laughing, in me.

That light, undimmed, burns still, casting a small light amidst the enlarged shadows of was, is, may be, could be, and never. That light is the light we all see when the noise dies down; it is stillness, the sharp relief of early dawn, the newness of each day, time in all its futile ticking and marking of what can never be wholly captured. Light and dark, fire unquenched, day and night and day again, and I am all I was promised I never would be, more than I could have imagined, unbounded in a world built on ties and tethers. This is the light of the spheres, and by it we see ourselves, not through the eyes of others, but as we truly are, and all that we could ever be. A universe in miniature, every cell a mirror, every possibility a reality, not woman, beyond body, not she. Me.

Philippa Brown, *Carnival of Resistance*

"Zoe is a Cunt" *Reflections on Researching Violence*

By Zoe John

Zoe John is a PhD researcher at Cardiff University's School of Social Sciences. Her work explores the production and management of violence and gender in mixed martial arts (MMA). Zoe uses a flexible researcher role to participate in MMA classes for research purposes, noting on her own experiences of felt, suggestive, and observed experiences.

1.   Field note

I sat there, looking, the pen in my mouth, chewing it as I watch the class. Coach came over and stared at me for a bit. "Alright Sherlock?" he mimics smoking a pipe. So do I. —I laughed while he stared at me for several more seconds before continuing; "Heh, normally a cock."

2.   Field note

I sat down on one of the benches with my notebook, preparing to write. The coach comes over "you jumping in?"
  "No got a big game on Saturday".
  "Got any baddies?"
  "Nah, just knackered."
  Coach: "Nobody cares."
A few second pass while he continued to stare. He pretends to suck a penis.

3.   Field note

I readjusted my sports bra before we started. It can really dig into me so obviously, uncomfortable. At that moment coach is standing beside me, and mimics adjusting breasts on himself and laughs. I look around the other women in confusion. "Hey! They get sweaty and out of place, okay? Let me have my moment to sort it out …" Sarah joins the conversation: "I can confirm is annoying." Coach then continues to rub his legs in a creepy manner, licking his lips while doing so.

4.   Field note

In between rounds, I was standing with one hand on my hip and one hand on the side of the cage. I was tired. Coach, walking on the outside of the cage while there was a break: "Very nice. How much?"

5.   Field note

Today I was taking part in the first class. I was punching on the bag. "Zoe is a cunt, Zoe is a cunt," he sings in a very melodic tune.

The last three to four years I've been conducting research becoming a mixed martial artist (MMA). The main aims of this research were to explore how fighters learn the practice of MMA, how they define violence, as well as how they 'become' members of their clubs in general. Though fighters praised the controlled aspects of violence in MMA, with rules, regulations, and abilities to fight a display skill as opposed to emotion, 'violence' was still being experienced and used in different ways.

Numerous jokes, forms of humiliation, as well as symbolic/semiotic violence were used to construct how fighters are expected to practice (and belong) in that particular space. From observations, to interviews, to reviews of online MMA forums, these spaces were overwhelmingly filled with misogynistic, homophobic, and sexist narratives, many of which were also explicitly said to me during observations—as the small example of field notes express. From the 'tyrannies', to the 'fags', the 'cunts' the 'sluts', such terms highlight who aren't meant or welcome to belong, who are different, or 'Other'—not just for women, but for men too.

In my limited years of research prior to the PhD, I naively thought that these were moments I wouldn't experience as a researcher or MMA practitioner (after all… those lengthy and detailed ethical consent applications were approved…). I often felt sad, angry, scared, frustrated, though I would try to give off a sense of confidence by laughing off these situations. It was tiring.

Importantly, these jokes and experiences continually highlighted a reminder to me of the potential danger. I was vulnerable, I was a minority, and

I felt like a failure as a researcher to not want to be there. Did the coach *actually* find me sexually attractive? Am I in danger? What must be exchanged in order to truly be considered part of that space? Is this done specifically to me as a researcher, as a woman, or both? I am unsure how long would I have stayed if not for the sense of obligation to research.

This entry is a small reflection from my accounts which I am still reliving, re-thinking. I am still trying to analyse its purpose both relative to the sporting context, my body, my field notebook. I am still accounting for the severity, the frequency, and how such overlooked moments or 'jokes' are harrowing, are controlling (and apparent definitions of masculinity for the fighters, too). Importantly, the accounts of the 'researcher' is not a unified or uncomplicated position, and the experiences of women (and 'others') in field must continue to be realised, to be discussed, and accounted for in more critical ways. So too must we discuss the ways in which we define violence, how we experience forms of violence in day-to-day life, and how we can challenge such forms to progress not only in sport and research, but broader societal contexts.

It is not enough to pass over these experiences as 'just a joke'. These moments matter and they are also *of* matter for analysis and critique.

From an academic stance to the everyday mundane situation, there is much more to be done.

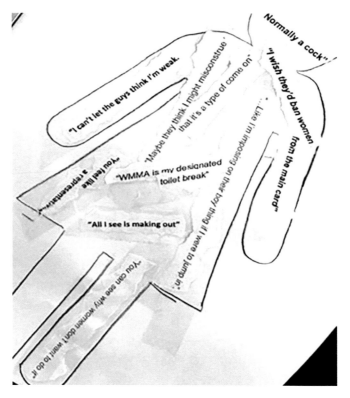

Zoe John, *Fighting Phallusy*

The image expresses a state of emotion and anxiety while analysing data from ethnographic research on becoming a mixed martial artist (MMA). Forms of data included interviews, field note observations, and online forums— all overwhelmingly filled with misogynistic and sexist narratives (with many explicitly said to myself as researcher and participant). Through ripping and cutting these harsh words, the visual representation of the comments aided analytical themes, but also my own agitations. It is but a small example of the harsh reality of women's positionality as researchers, but also, the experiences of women in MMA (and sport) in general.

Richard Blacklaw Jones, *Planet Bo Zo: One Rule For You*

Working in a Factory during Covid

By John Frost

Working in a factory during Covid has shown me first-hand how little prepared the government and the food Industry was for a viral pandemic and how cheap working-class and migrant lives are to the Capitalist system.

In the past, if someone had said to me that I would be working in a factory during a viral pandemic and there would be a nationwide lockdown in order to suppress that virus I would have laughed and dismissed such an obscene prediction. It's not that I look down on such work, which I understand is necessary to the manufacturing of mass goods, especially food for a substantial population nor that I view myself above such work; I come from a proud Welsh working-class background and I have often undertook manual work in agriculture; and although I was well read on threats registered on the government's National Risk Register, I would have justified my laughter on two counts: firstly, like most people my age, I was carefree and would not have acknowledged such turmoil ahead in my personal life. Secondly, I assumed, despite my disdain of the Conservative Party, that the government and the public health institutions would be competent in its response to protect its citizens from such a threat; thus such an outbreak would be controlled from the onset and suppression of a virus through a nationwide lockdown would not be required. Poignantly, I was wrong on both counts and the prediction would have been accurate. Alas, I unfortunately find myself and my fellow workers in this position.

To begin, I think it is important to outline a little of my personal background and how I began working at a factory, to add context. After leaving a full-time caring role of a dear loved one late last year due to their untimely passing, I found myself unemployed. Transferring from Carers Allowance to Universal Credit meant I was plunged into instant poverty that had me relying on foodbanks and handouts from family and friends. Despite my grief, I immediately began applying for jobs. With a top degree from a Russell Group University along with a well-developed CV. I was hopeful to find a new job quickly and secured two interviews. The time is late February 2020. News had filtered in December 2019 and January about a novel coronavirus epidemic in China and then in February a fast-developing pandemic with an outbreak in Northern Italy. I was hopeful that the UK government was hard at work planning to contain the virus. Tragically, I was wrong.

The time is March. I fall ill with suspicious symptoms: a temperature; tight chest; fatigue; headache. I assume its Covid-19. I cannot obtain a test (unless I pay an astronomical fee for a private test) because there is no mass testing. There is no track and trace system. I am worried about people I have been in contact with, so I contact them. There is no lockdown. Most do not isolate: the desperate need to work; ignorance; even selfishness. One job interview is postponed, and one is outright cancelled. I am sick for two weeks; worried about my finances, how I will pay my bills, how I will get a job and worst of all watching a disaster unfolding in my country. I recover. I emerge from self-isolation to a nationwide lockdown. The economy is frozen apart from key worker roles. So, I apply for supermarket vacancies. I hear nothing back. I sign up with an agency and get told to come to an induction for factory work the next day. As a worker, with nothing to sell but my labour, bills to pay and a nationalist urge to help my country through the crisis (not business owners or the Capitalist economy but the people) I oblige.

On inspection, I hope we can see some criticisms of the government's handling of the pandemic. Bluntly, lack of testing; lack of track and trace infrastructure; and failure to lockdown sooner has undoubtedly cost lives. (Along with the PPE fiasco and lack of quarantine measures for international arrivals). However, now I want to turn attention to my experience of working in the factory during and post-lockdown, and how failures by the government and the factory led to a localised outbreak. Importantly, I write this full of discontent for how the Welsh working class and migrant worker's lives have been undervalued. But, also with a little hope, that my writings may influence the government and factories, especially in the food industry, that measures must be taken to prevent another localised outbreak and a second wave of Covid-19 so workers, their loved ones and their communities are protected.

It is late March and Wales is locked down. I begin work in the cleaning team. In fairness, the factory has adopted some good social distancing measures. For example: announcements have been put up in different languages warning of the novel coronavirus, how it spreads and key symptoms; announcements have been put up encouraging good hygiene; tables have been removed from the canteen and chairs limited; markers put on the floor for queuing and a two way system introduced; tents have been placed outside to prevent overcrowding; different sections of the factory have been allocated different breaks to prevent the canteen becoming crowded; barriers have been put up on the production line to separate workers. It seems impressive. But, if only the factory took such a competent approach to PPE. Perhaps it was cost? Perhaps there was a shortage? But, surely there should be stores of PPE at a food factory in case of a pandemic? Obviously not. I worked from the end of March until early May in standard PPE which included a workwear overall and hair net. No face masks or visors were provided. I am not an epidemiologist and perhaps during lockdown, when the virus is being suppressed, it was safe for a lack of PPE however the localised outbreak that proceeded as soon as society started to reopen proves PPE should have already been provided and in constant use. The upcoming localised outbreak in the factory was going to infect a substantial number of workers, including this writer.

The time is May. Due to zero-hour contracts, despite my hard work and never missing a shift, one day the supervisor informed me there were too many workers on site and I was to leave. Consequently, I would not work for three weeks and heard nothing from the agency until the end of May. I return and work for one week in a different department; still no face masks are worn despite rumours that workers had been off sick and had tested positive for coronavirus. Similarly, one day on the second week I get told the same dreaded line: "there are too many workers on site, leave." I have no work for two weeks but in the middle of June I get a call asking me to work. I return and there is a dramatic transformation with PPE; finally, workers walk around in face visors. The rumours had been true and apparently even more workers had been off sick. I ask for my PPE. I get told it will come soon. The same *question and answer* goes on for days, with different supervisors in different departments because I am moved around daily to plug labour gaps. I consider walking out but I am worried about my finances and due to the insecure nature of the work, being labelled a "troublesome worker" and never getting a phone call from the agency again. I work for two weeks without proper PPE. It is Tuesday 24th June 2020. I feel tired and dehydrated. I finish my shift. I leave the factory and my eyes are red and painful. I cannot open my eyes for five minutes. Instinctively, I order a Covid test from the government website despite not having the traditional symptoms but due to my suspicions. My suspicions are proved correct; I test positive for Covid-19 on 26th June.

Thankfully, I have recovered from this terrible disease. However, I felt compelled to write this piece because I am concerned: one, another worker may not be as lucky as me and two, the government and factories need to competently prepare for a second wave. Therefore, I want to now outline what I think can be done to prevent a future outbreak. Unacceptably, I have read factory officials and the government attempt to divert blame onto workers. For example, they have suggested workers failed to social distance and continued to share car rides; failed to wear PPE; and some worked regardless of knowingly having covid-19 symptoms. Whereas some of these claims may be true it does not absolve the factory nor the government of responsibilities or blame; such behaviours need understanding especially from a Leftist perspective. Specifically, I argue these behaviours can be changed if economic conditions are modified. But, firstly the most obvious recommendation which is the responsibility of the factory: there needs to be a constant stockpile of full PPE. This needs to be demanded by trade unions and legislated by government. You cannot blame workers like me for failing to wear the PPE when we are not issued any!

Secondly, I recommend regular mass testing of the whole factory. Again, I am surprised it took an outbreak for this to happen. Importantly, this will allow infected people like myself who did not have a fever (worker's temperatures are rightly taken with a laser thermometer before we enter the site) or who are asymptomatic to be found. But it is fundamental here to note this offers the company an easy solution. To be clear, I fully support mass regular testing, but this must be backed up with economic measures that protect workers. For example, because I caught Covid, I missed out on two weeks of full pay. Instead, I was paid measly £198 of statutory sick pay. In addition, I have a second cash in hand job (simply because I cannot survive on the minimum wage factory job) which I work on the weekends which I could not attend. But I did not display typical symptoms; I never displayed a fever and I could easily have bypassed the temperature reading and continued to work. I chose not to because I care about others, and I did not want to spread this virus further. However, I know first-hand poverty and I understand why, if some workers have mild symptoms (or none), they would choose to work through it. Irresponsible? Arguably yes but is it not also irresponsible we have created an economy where workers are punished for simply being sick? Again, I am shocked there has been no thought to how workers can be protected economically. But I am actually being naive; the Conservative Party is highly class conscious and could not care less about worker's pay. Regardless, I propose progressive measures to take away financial pressure and accordingly reward workers for their tireless hard work that allows the food industry to function. Hence, I suggest: wage increases; free public transport (because another example of a financial loss I suffered was on the Monday before I fell sick I paid £28.00 for a weekly bus ticket. I used it for two days before I had to self-isolate. I called Stagecoach and requested a refund stating the circumstances however this was dismissed by the company); rent breaks and full pay if someone tests positive.

Before I sum up, I would like to write about migrant workers who have a different experience at the factory and in Welsh society than me. The workforce is diverse and apart from Welsh/English workers (of course English workers should be considered migrants however due to cultural hegemony I would argue they are far less likely to suffer from xenophobia) there are migrants from: Ireland; Portugal; Brazil; East Timor; Philippines; Bulgaria; Romania and Poland. To be clear: without the hard work, dedication and reliability of migrant workers, the factory and the food industry would not function. Despite this, I have witnessed racism at the factory and in society generally during the pandemic. As noted, the factories' subtle attempt to place blame on the workers for the localised outbreak can also be argued to be rooted in Xenophobia. This narrative places blame on migrant workers whom often live in large households; cannot afford to miss work due to financial pressure here and often in their home country and a general fear of losing their jobs (and arguably due to their vulnerable position at this time during the rise in Xenophobic nationalism and the hardening of the Conservative Right). However, these workers should not be blamed for their situation.

In addition, I already felt close to migrants due to our shared social class, but I feel even closer to their plight since experiencing agency work. For example, I vividly recall during the 2016 EU referendum the argument used by the populist right that migrant workers undercut the Welsh working class. Actually, this is incorrect and is used to divert attention away from lack of regulation and ruthless exploitative measures. For example, as an agency worker, I am on significantly lower wages than workers employed by the factory. However, the factory is not hiring, and the only available work is through the agency. Therefore, the agency is actively undercutting, and migrants have no other choice but to go through them. This infuriates me. British Capitalism is an exploitative society for both the Welsh working class and migrants, yet it is the migrants who are blamed for it. The Left in Wales must counter this narrative and there is no better time than now when migrant labour has been so indispensable. For a start, the Trade Unions should become more combative. I appropriate some blame to USDAW, the designated union. Conceivably, USDAW allows such conditions to exist unchallenged, attempts none whatsoever to challenge this narrative and makes zero attempts to recruit migrants. Despite concerns for their own safety, migrants have continued to work hard and tirelessly, and along with the Welsh working class and deserve recognition, support and inclusion.

Overall, I am shocked about the government's abysmal response to the protection of its citizens, and I am equally angry about it and the factories' lack of planning and care for the protection of workers. From my article, I hope you can see why my anger is justified. I wish there will be no second wave and it will simply fizzle away after being suppressed. But sadly, as I speak outbreaks are being reported again across Europe and a catastrophe is currently ongoing in the USA and Brazil. The food factory environment shows coronavirus thrives indoors; in a cold, crowded environment which suggests the winter period could be even more deadly. Johnson says he does not want to lockdown again but if there is no active learning from fundamental past mistakes then we will have no choice. On that note, I urge you to join me to demand that health and economic measures are taken to protect food factory workers, their families, and the surrounding communities from such a ruthless enemy. These workers keep us fed; we must keep them safe.

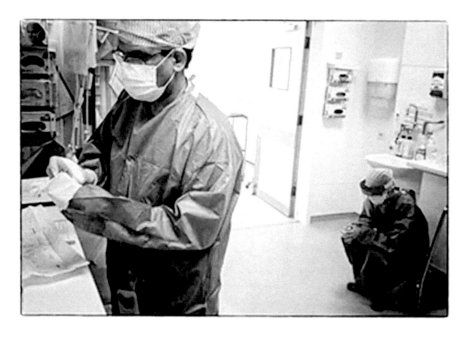

David Collyer, *All in a Day's Work*

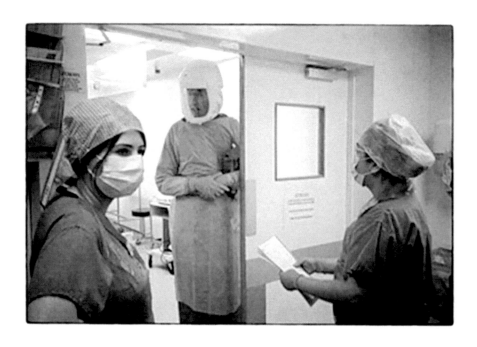

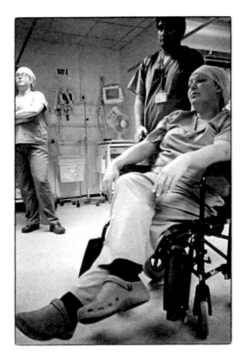

David Collyer, *All in a Day's Work*

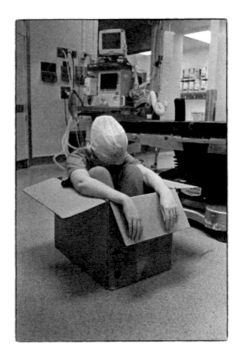

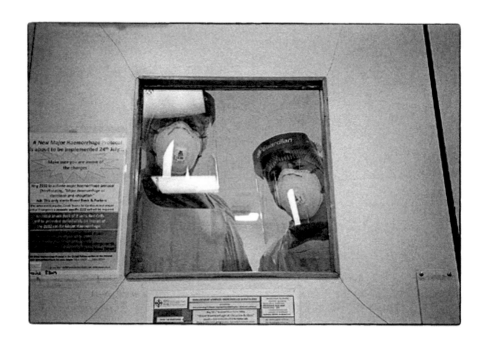

David Collyer, *All in a Day's Work*

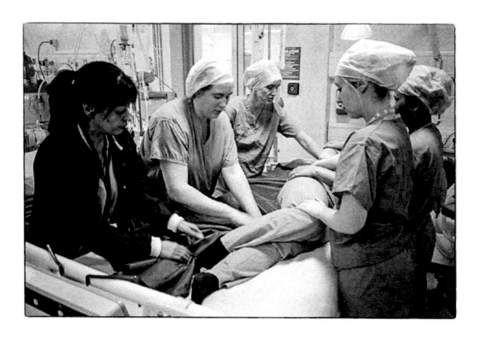

Breath Play

By Rhys Trimble

A pulmonary embolism (PE) is a blood clot on the lung. I suffered this illness on the 1st of May. As I got into the car around 11:30 pm I was overcome with a coughing fit which in the dark I thought had produced a little sputum but as I drove home from my friend's house, I could see the redness of blood droplets glinting on the windscreen. I called NHS direct and eventually was phoned by an out-of-hours doctor who recommended that I didn't drive and phone an ambulance if symptoms worsened. Having coughed up more blood in the early hours of Sunday morning I phoned an ambulance. In attendance around 10:20 am on the 2nd of May "Beth" the paramedic after examining me said that I should drive myself to the hospital because my symptoms where not severe enough to be taken in by ambulance. After some very poor driving I entered A&E where I queued and admitted myself. I stood for much of my wait offering my seat to elderly patients who had been there since 2 a.m the previous night. I say the paramedic Beth at the desk who avoided my gaze. This was 11:20 am Sunday morning, after I was seen I situated myself in the corridor that ran behind triage. I was reading a novel "Ceiliog Dandi" a fictionalized comedy novel about Dafydd ap Gwilym. Other times I wrote into my notebook, thoughts and overheard speech:

DI FESUR   *lle ti'n do di fewn* STOP BEATHING..BREATH AWAY..

SUH..SUH..

INCIDENT STAFF what's occurring byrbennu

sylla a gofoddela!

call iawn canula

IODINE DYE look up   borderline

gweld bloodforms

understood   *wnai...*

sgidiau, sannau a trowsys ,   thyroxin

what should i expect?   *Eglwys dydd Sul*
passivity—*a mydr*   *"OGYDD" Achosion brys*
dim byd i'w fwyta   "Ocê dol" secondment na
paid paid nightshift   greener on the other side
with my eyes shut   *brêc di, brêc ia, bod yma?*
rhywyn wrth y drws   David Jones: chest pains

Rhwng y cwn a'r brain -------brain-fever

budr-waith shellac   chart pancake

whistle dixie   inhale

                chwistl dwr

        a quickened float, shrewish

                beside marble

    a late   turn

                foot ear math

    fingering change

            lipping beanie

    b&w topknot

    besicles & bascular

                wood:not nice

    shan't i shan't

    shunning..

_____

sylla a gofoddela!: look on in wonderment!
sgidiau, sannau a trowsys: Shoes, socks and trousers
Eglwys dydd Sul: Sunday School Church

brêc di, brêc ia, bod yma?: A break is a break being here?
rhywyn wrth y drws: Someone by the door
Rhwng y cwn a'r brain: between the dogs and the crows

paper lounge

        Llanddulas

            black /blue

After various opinions being given by doctors and the shifts changing over, I was to get a CT scan of my lungs. The recorded voice said: STOP BREATHING [10seconds] then BREATHE AWAY…After nightmarish night in Gogarth ward I was told I was to be put on anitcoagulents then left without receiving the medication for 4 hours. A nurse Tom finally went to look for the apixaban which was not brought up for an unexplained reason. I had received my first AZ vaccine on 22nd April. Asking consultant Dr Azzu about the implications of the vaccine he assured me that a study was being done "somewhere in England" and my data may be added to that study. I discovered independently that it is possible to be tested to check interactions between the AZ vector-based vaccine and platelets but there was no mention of a test being carried out. I received the Pfizer as a second dose of C19 vaccine. I am still on apixaban. Betsi Cadwaladr Health board was taken off on 'special measures' in November 2020 as it had been since June 2015 but was put on similar though differently worded intervention plan in March 2021. Its levels of service are still below average. Stop breathing…breathe away.

Rachel Oliver, *No one voted for this Shambles*

Alba gu bràth   Don't give up Hoping Hannah

By Gwenno Dafydd

(Alba gu brath x 4)
I saw you weeping
Outside the seat of power
(Alba gu brath)
As you reflected
On Scotland's wilting flower
A new horizon
Was all that really mattered
But dawn had broken
As dreams and hopes lay shattered
(Alba gu brath x2)
The eye of the storm
Grew Wednesday in the Meadows
The troops were gath'ring
As Alba's future led us
Sing Freedom's Anthem
Small nations join together
We shall be heard
Our chains released forever.
Alba gu brath

Chorus
Don't give up hoping Hannah
Don't despair
The winds of change are blowing
And a gale is on its way
A sea of saltires
Were sailing in the sky
All proudly saying 'Aye'.
Alba gu brath x 2

Close to success
A bright new future rising
Lies and deceit
From traitors was surprising
You showed the way
And gave us inspiration.
The seeds are sown
To once more be a nation.
Alba gu bràth

Chorus

Instrumental

A Alba gu bràth.
No footsteps we can follow
A Alba gu bràth.
We can create tomorrow.
A Alba gu bràth,
Sailing unchartered waters.
A Alba gu bràth.
For all our sons and daughters. (X 2 all the way through again).
Don't give up hoping Hannah.

Alba gu bràth *is a Scottish Gaelic phrase used to express allegiance to Scotland. Translated into English it means "Scotland forever", literally "Scotland until judgment." The phrase is often used as a political slogan in the campaign for Scottish independence. The final part of the song comes directly from a speech given by Nicola Sturgeon in around 2011.*

My Rough Guide to Being a Human

By Caroline Richards

It's wholly appropriate when we focus on the wrong in the world but it's important to acknowledge the good stuff too—so can I just take this moment to say, *I fucking love being alive.*

And more than that, I love being *old* and alive. Being older rocks. Being older gives you a stronger sense of belonging, of understanding, we can identify with more people because we've been more ages and had more close conversations with a wider variety of people. We've had chance to make more mistakes and to understand them, we've had chance to work out what's important to us. And one of the best bonuses is watching generations grow! Seeing toddlers with family resemblances mature into new beings, understanding the pains and tribulations that all families go through, knowing we're all connected through them, knowing you're never the worst, best, most of anything ... there'll always be someone more extreme than you—with one exception and we know what that is, yeah? No-one can be a better version of you than you—how extraordinary it is that we're all guaranteed to be the best at something, so let's turn it into an art. Let's start living our life as the one-off creation it is, our most complex creation, a multi-dimensional masterpiece of layers and correlations, interspersed with pinnacles of emotion and achievements.

So, if you're approaching 30 and feeling like it's the peak of Pen-y-fan, don't fret! There's a much bigger world out there and you're just about to discover how much richer life can get. And I don't mean to bang on but here's some advice I wish I'd believed when I eased my way into adulting.

Number one—don't pigeon-hole yourself. Plenty of others will do that for you, please don't do it to yourself. You can be anything so aim in any direction you goddamn want. Try everything, learn anything—who knows how far you'll fly if you start investing now. Have patience—reaching a dream is an awesome achievement at any age, joining a band in ten years' time will be just as cool as it is now. Broaden your life experiences, develop those skills, feel inspired, get excited, feel connected, inspire others, feel fuckin awesome and share it.

2. Remember all decision-making can be boiled down to acting from fear or acting from love. Try to swing the balance in the direction you want to head. Self-love is as important as caring for others. Martyr and Mater sound similar because they're nearly the same thing. Being a parent is the most important job in the world but love yourself too. Also, there's nothing heroic about being a martyr to adults ... they'll never grow up if you don't let them.

3. Embrace your features, your shape, your size—own your body and love it. Appreciate it every day for getting you about as well as it does. Physical bodies are wonderful things—all of them, not just size medium. Find out what your body will do—stretch it, pump it, balance it, dance it, get it mucky, get it salty, thank it, rest it and do it some more.

4. Remember everyone can draw, sing, dance, and type.

5. Our planet is not just for human convenience—meet Nature halfway.

6. Find good role models.

7. Always find time to do what you love and not just what you feel you should.

Let's end with infinity, number 8. A healthy world needs wonderful humans. Stick up for yourself and for others too, find your power and use it for good. The Universe is on side, not everything needs micromanaging and there's more than one way to do everything. Aim to engage not control; keep the faith don't fret; never give up just breathe and show up, the rest will happen, the world keeps turning regardless—so let's flex our bodies, relax our souls, and enjoy this goddamn ride of our lives.

Afterword

By Prof. K.E. Howell

'Time must be brought to light and genuinely grasped as the horizon of every understanding and interpretation of being.' —Martin Heidegger

As Heidegger writes, we are all becoming as we shuffle along this mortal coil of life, and stories such as these, ensure that we are reminded of our common, cultural *being*, whilst at the same time, the individuality of our narratives, reminds us of our *self*, in this rich tapestry of life.

Within these pages you'll find an immediacy in Welsh culture that cannot be ignored.

Land of Change: Stories of Struggle & Solidarity gives a flavour of not only *being* in Wales, but also *being* in the world, and captures a sense of both *being* and *becoming*. Not only concerned with the individual, *becoming* resonates far deeper within our collective cultural experience and social existence. This anthology therefore illustrates a historical and contemporary view of Wales, underlining a critical theory perspective, as well as issues related to path-dependency in the developing lives of individuals as well as society.

Many of the experiences found in this anthology take me back to a different time, but within each story an immediacy remains firmly within the present. Growing up in the 1970s and 80s on a Welsh council estate in Caerphilly, I left school at 16 without any qualifications, and worked in factories: at one point I was bailing cardboard. Eventually, I went to London where I experienced many different people, and many different viewpoints. I worked as a kitchen porter, waiter and barperson but eventually ended up on the buildings and on returning to Wales, I undertook a short apprenticeship to become a bricklayer. I worked on various building sites and found the work interesting at times (there were worse jobs), but I always felt a sense of alienation and demoralisation.

I had always read extensively, but this was undirected, so I decided to study for a couple of O Levels (GCSEs) and a number of WEA courses at the local college. Whilst doing this, a few avenues were pointed out to me and eventually, I applied to a mature student College in Wales called Coleg Harlech. My two years there, studying Literature and History, proved to be the best time of my life, and following a rejection from Oxford to study PPE, I read Politics and Philosophy at Cardiff University. Luckily, I then won funding to do a PhD, became an academic and have remained in Higher Education ever since. Working in HE was not easy and numerous struggles needed to be overcome, but I recognised I was lucky, and others were not so fortunate.

In the opening story 'Working-class Woman,' Rhoda Thomas' account of the struggles faced by working-class women resonates not only because it captures the many barriers faced by the working classes, but also because there is a level of optimism in her observation that "joining together with others is the most powerful instrument for change." Spending most of her life in Wales, trying to make a living through teaching and continually worried about finances, Rhoda explains how through struggle (an ideal endowed by her parents), she questioned the flaws in the system but even in the face of deprivation, she continued to develop both herself and those around her.

Mark S. Redfern's article, 'When Vice Came to Swansea,' explores the notion of poverty-porn, in relation to a negative depiction of the Welsh working class. He rightly investigates the failure to look beneath the surface and dig deeper to provide an authentic message—a more sincere recognition of Welsh culture in the wider world. Even though 'vice' is an aspect of existence, Welshness is far more pervasive and meaningful than this!

The recognition of the ongoing debate regarding the nature of communism and Marxism as a means of countering imperialism (which informed my political education) is made explicit with 'The Battle of Trafalgar Square' by Tim Evans, and Tim Richards' personal account of the Miners' Strike, as it is in the destruction of working-class monuments (Phil Knight's 'Struggle on the Wall'), and Leon Noakes (whose uncle Noakesy I knew well) turns to independence, based on "a new spirit in Welsh culture and the creation of the Welsh Assembly."

At my core, I am still a valley boy from a council estate: this is the bedrock of who I am and colours my very essence. Like all of us, I was thrown into my existence, and we are all in a state of *becoming* in a world that we could not define, nor choose. We are thrust into our culture and society at a particular time in history, and we must make sense of who we are.

For Wales as a nation, this has meant a level of subordination, made explicit by the harsh lessons of the 1980s. Of course, historical events have sculpted who we are and the formation of the Senedd (formerly the Welsh Assembly) in the early 21st Century, which has provided the basis for a Wales with self-determination. In this respect, the Senydd itself is in a process of *becoming*, and at its core, has a path-dependency that carries with it a Welsh identity, and cultural perspectives built on values of equality, fraternity, independence, liberty, and social democracy.

Providing a framework to enable a direction which can lead to us *becoming*, the Senydd has given the Welsh a more informed understanding of ourselves in the world. The narratives in this anthology underscore such understandings, highlighting an array of individual experiences which represent culture in its entirety. Welsh literature and art reflect Welsh lives, and each contribution provides a means by which we can gauge our own experiences as aspects of a wider existence and cultural embodiment.

As a product of Welsh education, and now as a Professor of Governance, I believe that ***Land of Change: Stories of Struggle & Solidarity from Wales*** captures the notion of *becoming* within a Welsh and wider context, and from a phenomenological perspective it develops rationales for political awareness in everyday existence; helping us to understand the bric-a-brac of daily life.

We need more narratives such as these, and I commend each of the authors, artists, photographers, and the editor, as well as **Culture Matters** for ensuring these individual stories are brought to life. Each of the narratives resonate throughout time, as well as within the specific characteristics of daily existence in Wales, recognising the essence of dissent; from the tradition of the bard, right through to the right to write, question and protest.

However, it is important to note, that within this anthology, each story and artwork involves an understanding of *self* through *others*, and the associated collective suffering and striving that underlies the veneer of our existence. In this sense, it is imperative to ensure that our communal story is told, especially when it underpins "the horizon of every understanding and interpretation of being" and is integral to the development of identity, culture and *becoming* in Wales and beyond.

Cadfloedd Rhyddid

Freedom's War Cry

Clywch yr udgorn-floedd i'r rhyfel
Yr dyrwygo bron yr awel;
Duwies Rhyddid eilw'r uchel
Ar ei phlant I'r gad:
Gormes gyda'I lu arglwyddi
Sydd yn chwifio eu baneri:
Nawr ney byth, wroniaid Cymru,
Awn i'r gad, i'r gad;
Dawrder ein cyndeidiau
Enyn ein mynwesau,
Megys tân, i'n gyru'n mlaen
Nes mynu ein hiawnderau:
Os gorchfygir nig an ormes.
Na foed neb i ddweyd yr hanes;
Marw'n wrol wnawn ar fynwes
Rhddid yn y gad.

Daniel James

Contributor Biographies

Rhoda Thomas is a radical poet, based in Swansea, where she lives with her partner and two cats. Originally from London, she has been settled in Wales for 40 years, contributing to the training of social workers, counsellors and doctors as a psychologist and sociologist. She has held office in student and trade unions and with Tim Evans, she convenes the annual Llanelli 1911 Railway Strike Commemoration Festival, which is fast becoming a regular fixture in the trade union calendar. She is a founder member of Live Poets Society, which brings together poets from across south Wales for workshops and open-mic events. A member of the Socialist Workers Party, she gives talks and writes on subjects such as the lives of female revolutionaries and the damage to our health from the food industry. She reads regularly at poetry groups and events. She is the author of 'Survive and grow in difficult times,' and her poetry can be found in recent anthologies, in *Red Poets*, and in her poetry collections. In this prose-piece she writes about the challenges she has faced in life as a working-class woman, and the value of solidarity.

Arron Kuiper is an artist practicing in North Wales. He began developing his singular technique of sculptural painting in 2006, which he continues to perfect to this day. His work has been featured in publications like *a.n. Magazine*, *Vice* and *Business Insider*, and has been displayed in various galleries around the UK including the Discerning Eye, Cardiff Contemporary and BEEP Wales. He also occasionally sells some art.

Alan Perry is a poet, painter and short-story writer living and working in Swansea. A past winner of the Eric Gregory Award for Poetry, he is the author of some 10 books of poetry and stories and a contributor to Parthian's anthology *Poetry 1900-2000*, a collection of a hundred poets of Wales of the 20th century. His work has been broadcast on radio and television and has appeared in a wide range of books, magazines and periodicals, notably *LMNTRE Poems* by Vernon Watkins and *From Aberfan to Grenfell* (which he illustrated, in collaboration with Mike Jenkins.). His documentary book on homelessness in Swansea, *Music You Don't Normally Hear*, was widely praised when it came out and was later adapted (by Perry) for the stage and was produced in Swansea and later in Cardiff, directed by Karl Francis. Together with Aida Birch and his wife Jean, he was a founder member and trustee of the Terry Hetherington Award to Young Writers and together with Costa Award-winning poet Jonathan Edwards has edited a number of the Award's annual anthologies. His latest collection of poems is *Waters* and was selected as a *Wales Arts Review* Welsh Book of the Decade. He has been married for 55 years to portraitist and painter Jean Perry and they have two grown-up sons who are also artists.

Mark S. Redfern is an investigative journalist with voice.wales, an unashamedly working-class grassroots media organisation, born in Swindon and now writing from Powys. Mark won *Planet's* 2019 Young Writers' Essay Competition. In his winning essay he argues that a globally popular Vice documentary, repackaged for YouTube, gives a condescending and sensationalist angle on Swansea's heroin crisis, has left a poisonous legacy in capturing for posterity humiliating depictions of the protagonists, and has misrepresented working-class Welsh culture. This essay subsequently won the 2020 Wales PEN Cymru Emyr Humphreys Award.

Bronwen Davies has emerged fresh in 2022 with a new music project, DJ'ing as Hertz-2-luv, mixing heavy sounds of jungle, rap and atmospheric drum and bass. Home and her natural environment in Cwmbach have become the foundation for Bronwen's work, both as a quiet retreat for creative reflection and a sanctuary from the unnatural impositions and unpredictable nature of society. In her surroundings it is possible to be free to explore either through creativity in her home recording studio or by spending time in Nature.

Jacqueline Jones grew up in rural West Wales. Her parents ran a bakery. She has had a variety of occupations from film extra to working on factory production lines. She has exhibited her art worldwide, and most recently at The Mall Galleries. She is a member of the art movement Stuckism and has formed an offshoot movement called Rural Punk. Her art comes directly out of her life and what she's experiencing. She believes that elitism has no place in the making of art, only quality. Jacqueline lives in a working-class area, and she draws a lot on inner resources to make art. To Jacqueline, art is like breathing, and 'something I need to do every day.'

Tony Webb was born and bred in the East Side region of Swansea, 'where its industrial heartland was'. He attended Cwm Junior School and Cefn Hengoed School in Winchwen/Bonymaen and was hopeless at all subjects except English. He wrote his first story at the age of 10. His work has been widely published. He is also a vocalist/guitar player and singer in the well-known Swansea Folk/Rock band Sparrow Lane. He is a committed socialist who would like to see an independent socialist Wales.

Phil Knight is a poet and political activist. He joined CND as a teenager back in the 1980s and has been involved in many campaigns including Stop the War Movement, ANL, Stand Up to Racism and fighting against the sell-off of council houses. He is a member of the Socialist Worker Party. In 2015 the *Red Poets* published 'You are Welcome to Wales.' He is the MC of Cheval Neath Poems & Pints which raises funds for the Terry Hetherington Young Writers'

Award. Phil's been published in *Red Poets, Poetry Wales, Planet, Dial 174* and Culture Matters' anthology, *Ymlaen/Onward!*

Caroline Richards found herself sat at a Formica table in a village in Northern Thailand In 2018, freewriting for the first time in a class led by the queer Irish activist and poet, Cat Brogan. Since then, her drive to write and deliver has remained constant as a way of processing feelings and events. Aside from contributing to Cardiff's Spoken Word scene, Caroline enjoys a varied career encompassing community and visual arts, carnival, and circus. Her piece, 'Carnival of Change' has been used in the soundtrack in one of a series of short films made for Butetown Arts and Culture Association, released in August 2020. Caroline was born in Newport, Gwent and has lived in Maidstone, London, Cambodia, Vietnam and China for varying amounts of time, but generally feels settled living her life in Cardiff, Wales. Her favourite playmates are her non-binary mxus and their puppy-dog lurcher. Two grown up children and weekly samba practices are the icing on her cake.

Osian Grifford is an artist/illustrator/performer and workshop tutor from Llangeitho, Ceredigion, and is currently based in Cardiff where he studied the Illustration BA at CSAD. The images are from an illustrated poetry / story book that was written in the Rhondda Sports Centre with writer Mike Church and a small group of looked-after children of various secondary school ages, in the weeks leading up to lockdown. The book was to vaguely communicate the experience of the group's situation as individuals, but Storm Dennis had just struck the area, leaving many people homeless. Covid hit the Rhondda disproportionately hard in the early days, just after the storms. For a lot of people Covid was just another of a pile of gigantic worries lumped onto their day-to-day journeys towards being where they needed to be in the world.

Rachel Oliver is an artist, a term she has found difficult to say out loud, which is mad because all her life she has encouraged others to follow their passion and be what they strive to be. She has worked in the voluntary homeless sector for many years and has always used art to engage and inspire young people to be creative. Rachel has always been politically committed to advocating and encouraging young people to voice their opinions and speak out through the medium of art. She was born in Gower with a rebellious side, channelling her inner quirk with a passion for urban art, graffiti, photography, illustration and the use of colour and visual delight. About 10 years ago, at a time in her life when she felt she had no voice, Rachel rediscovered her passion for expressing herself through art, and developed her own unique style of multimedia digital collage which helped her to heal, to speak out, to glow and grow. Through her creative work she releases her thoughts, her worries: it's her therapy, her protest march, her rhythmic drum, her shout-out platform to what's wrong in the world, to be kind, to highlight current issues, and it is her release. Without art, life would be quite grey and dull. Exhibitions she's been involved in include: Empower me exhibition (g39cardiff); Habitats Exhibition Cardiff; Dancing with Demons Exhibition Bristol, Swansea art fayre at the Elysium gallery, Swansea open Glyn Vivian gallery; Create Emerging Artists finalist (2020 exhibition) at Creates Gallery and Ardent gallery Brecon exhibition.

Gwenno Dafydd has been a professional actress, singer and writer since 1980 working in television, radio, theatre, cabaret, Theatre in Education and concerts all over Europe, Los Angeles and New York, but predominantly in Wales. She has also had a parallel career in knowledge sharing since 1998 with a focus on Equality, Diversity and Leadership Coaching. She works globally by Zoom as a Master Public Speaking Coach and contributes extensively to global podcasts on a variety of subjects to do with management and women in the workplace. She is the author of *Stand up & Sock it to them Sister. Funny, Feisty Females* (Parthian Press 2016); a one woman show about Edith Piaf entitled *No Regrets* which was published in *One Woman One Voice* (Parthian Press 2000 & 2005); a stage play, about the Falklands War, entitled *Paying the full Whack*; numerous scripts for children in Theatre in Education productions; eight pieces of children's poetry published in the *Llyfrau Lloerig* (Bonkers Books) (Gwasg Carreg Gwalch) series; and *Santa ar Streic?* (*Santa on Strike?*) for BBC Radio Cymru.

Leon Noakes is co-founder of YesCymru, the campaign for Welsh independence. He has a postgraduate degree from the University of South Wales, and is the author of *Withdrawn Traces: Searching for the Truth About Richey Manic* (Penguin, 2019). Raised by a lifelong Trotskyist in the St. James community, Caerphilly, South Wales, he became an advocate of Welsh freedom from British institutions during the rise of New Labour, accepting that socialism could not be pursued under London rule.

Tracey Rhys is a Bridgend writer, artist and editor, originally from the Rhondda Fach. In 2020, she won the Poetry Archive's 'WordView' competition. Her first poetry collection, *Teaching a Bird to Sing* (Green Bottle Press), was the result of a Literature Wales New Writer's Award, which allowed her time to write about her relationship with her son, who has a diagnosis of Autism Spectrum Disorder. Tracey's poems on autism have featured as monologues in two professional theatre productions with Company of Sirens, and she has exhibited at the Senedd for Autism Awareness month. Tracey has published poetry, essays and short stories in *Poetry Wales, Planet: The Welsh Internationalist, New Welsh Review*, and others. She has work in *Poems from* *the Borders* (Seren), *Bloody Amazing!* (Dragon-Yaffle), *A470* (Arachne Press), *Gwrthryfel/Uprising* (Culture Matters) and *Cast a Long Shadow* (Honno). Tracey's visual art is concerned with memories from her childhood. She creates figurative representations of the working classes, often at protest, within the Welsh environment. Tracey is a member of the Silures Art Group.

Tim Richards is a retired FE lecturer from Abertridwr, who was branch secretary of the University and College Union at Coleg Glan Hafren in Cardiff and a leading Anti-Poll Tax activist. He was also editor of *Y Faner Goch* (*The Red Flag*) newspaper, the paper published by Cymru Goch, a small Welsh republican socialist party who argued for independence for Wales for decades. It was as a law lecturer that he first got involved in the Miners' Strike when he was asked to give legal advice to miners who had been arrested while picketing: he already knew NUM members from Nantgarw Coking Ovens from having supported them in their fight to keep the coking ovens open in the late 1970s. It was early on during the Strike that he discovered that the NUM needed to set up Miners' Support Groups to raise money and food, and the Rhymney Valley Miners' Support Group, covering the Nantgarw, Penallta and Bedwas lodges, was the first group to be set up.

Gerhard Kress moved to the UK in 1977 from another EU country. He has been made to feel at home, especially in Wales where he's lived for nearly 15 years. All this changed on the 16th June 2016 when, with four million other Europeans, he became a target of right-wing government policies based on a glorified opinion poll. This has affected him and, his family for the past four years. Gerhard is a qualified social worker and have mostly worked with people who have severe learning disabilities and older people with degenerative brain disease. He is a visual artist, musician, and a poet, and his recent exhibitions including Lock Down Exhibition I & II at The Attic and Arts Centre, Treforest and Musicians at Caffi Soar at the Welsh Centre in Merthyr Tydfil, a permanent exhibition of mostly Welsh musicians in large black and white prints.

Adam Johannes grew up in poverty on a council estate. For the last twenty years, he has been active in many causes including the Welsh peace movement, co-founding Cardiff People's Assembly, an anti-austerity network, and other activism around racism, environment, unemployment, and poverty. He self-defines as a revolutionary socialist in the tradition of Karl Marx, Rosa Luxemburg, William Morris, Peter Kropotkin and CLR James. He is the founder and coordinator of the Cardiff People's Assembly against Austerity.

Kate Cleaver is an Anglo-Indian writer studying for a PhD with Swansea University. She is researching the lives of ordinary people who found themselves incarcerated in the Briton Ferry Insane Asylum, Vernon House. She is creating stories and has found that linking her stories to historical fact is a way to bring people from the past to life. In 2019 she was longlisted for the New Welsh Writers' Award and has had a memoir published by Parthian in *Just So You Know*, and another in *Painting the Beauty Queens Orange: Women's Lives in the 1970s* (Honno Welsh Women's Press, 2021).

Neelufur Adam known as **Nelly Adam** aka **Queen Niche** was born in 1985 in London and raised in Cardiff. She's the eldest of 8 siblings and is of Kenyan and Indian heritage. She has a BSc in Biomedical Science and is CIPD qualified. She works in Human Resources in the NHS and has been a BLM activist since June 2020. Nelly is a Human Rights activist and has spoken to the Welsh Government in Senydd to address issues about statues in Wales, and to the United Nations to address current issues of racism in Wales. Nelly also leads and is the Race Equality Champion for Zero Racism Wales. She also sits contributes to the Royal College of Drama & Arts, the National Museum of Wales, the Socio-Economic Sub-Group for Welsh Government (REAP), the Welsh Army and NPTC College Group consultation groups to advise on diversity, inclusion and equality action some of which include.

Claudia Boes moved from Germany to the UK in 1999 and is a longstanding activist, academic, intersectional feminist and co-founder of Cardiff Sisters of Solidarity and Women's Strike Cymru. As an occupational therapist, with an interest in perinatal and postnatal care, Claudia implements her practical knowledge as a single parent to support vulnerable and marginalised women in their journey through motherhood. Having co-organised the highly successful Cardiff Sisters' March in 2017, she is driven to raise awareness of the detrimental effect of austerity on women, in particular black, working-class and disabled women. She passionately believes in working with others and making a difference to where you live and has led practical campaigns for accessible, affordable and inclusive spaces for women and non-binary people to meet and empower each other. Part of this was the highly successful pop-up Women's Art Centre hosted by Cathay's Community Centre in 2018. She is the Joint Women's Officer for Cardiff West Labour and is currently putting her energy into Fairwater, the community where she lives and brings up her daughters. During the pandemic, she was involved in coordinating the Fairwater & Pentrebane Mutual Aid efforts and has seen how the community has come together to help. More recently, she has worked with her neighbours to implement a play scheme to allow children to play safely outside and Benthyg /Repair Cafe Wales to set up the Fairwater Repair Café, which continues to go from strength to strength, promoting community and sustainable living.

Krystal S. Lowe is a Bermuda-born, Wales-based dancer, choreographer, writer, and director, creating dance theatre works for stage, public space, and film that explore themes of intersectional identity, mental health and wellbeing, empowering audiences toward introspection and social change. She's an artist dedicated to creating, performing, and producing projects to empower communities, promote the Welsh language, and connect her work in Wales with her home country, Bermuda. Recent credits include: *Good Things to Come* commissioned by National Dance Company Wales and Literature Wales for the Welsh Government's Wales in Germany 2021; *Somehow*, commissioned by Music Theatre Wales; *Complexity of Skin* commissioned by the Space for BBC's Culture in Quarantine; *Intersectional Identities* project, funded by Arts Council Wales, Welsh Government, and the National Dance Foundation of Bermuda; *The History of Us | Ein Hanes Ni*, funded by Wales Arts International and Bermuda Civic Ballet; *Presenting Individual Identities*, Clwstwr funded R&D project; and Beacons Development Award 2021 for *Seven*, funded by BFI Network Wales, Ffilm Cymru, and the National Lottery.

Rebecca Lowe is a journalist, poet, events organiser, and Quaker peace activist, based in Swansea, South Wales. Her climate emergency poem 'Tick, Tick' was a Bread and Roses Spoken Word 2020 Award winner. Her poetry has been featured on BBC Bristol, BBC Radio 4's Poetry Workshop and BBC Radio 3 and featured in many anthologies including *Red Poets, Blackheath Countercultural Review*, and **Culture Matters**' *Ymlaen/Onward!* anthology of radical Welsh poetry. Rebecca's most recent publications include *Blood and Water* published by The Seventh Quarry (2020) and *Our Father Eclipse*, published by Culture Matters (2021).

MJ is a single parent living in the Trethomas in the Rhymney valley. She has lost many friends and relatives during in the Covid-19 pandemic and is suffering with the effects of long Covid herself. She uses art as a source of escapism and a way to channel her emotions.

lloyd robson is a Cardiff-born Welsh writer currently living in Virginia, USA. He is responsible for the books *city & poems, edge territory, letter from sissi* (all published by blackhat); *cardiff cut, bbboing! & associated weirdness*, and *Oh Dad! A Search for Robert Mitchum* (all published by Parthian Books).

Eric Ngalle Charles is a Cameroon-born Wales based writer, poet, playwright, actor, and activist. He is currently a doctoral student at King's College London. Following the publication last year of his autobiography, *I, Eric Ngalle*, Eric was selected by Jackie Kay as one of the UK's top ten BAME writers. He was recently the special guest at the African Festival of Emerging Writers, Cardiff Seren Poetry Festival and his short film *Eric Ngalle: This is Not a Poem* is currently touring the UK.

Tim Evans was born in Llanelli and now lives in Swansea. He worked as a teacher and lecturer and was active in the National Union of Teachers (now the NEU) and the National Association of Teachers in Further and Higher Education (now the UCU). In 2011 he set up the Llanelli 1911 Rail Strike Commemoration Society, which annually marks the killing of protesters by Churchill's troops and the uprising that followed. He has written extensively on Welsh history, and co-runs Live Poets Society, a political poetry group based in Swansea. He's a revolutionary socialist and member of Swansea Socialist Workers Party. Tim is also a lifelong anti-racist, and activist in the Anti-Nazi League, Rock Against Racism, Stand Up to Racism and Love Music, Hate Racism. His work has appeared in *Planet, New Welsh Review, Red Poets, Poets on the Hill* and the *International Socialism Journal* (*ISJ*). His article on Welsh syndicalism and the Cambrian Combine Strike was published in the *ISJ* in 2021. His latest poetry collection *Bones of the Apocalypse* was published by Frequency House in 2021.

Gemma June Howell is a grass-roots activist, writer, poet, tutor, academic, Associate Editor for **Culture Matters** and regular contributor to Nation Cymru. Founder of the CSOS, she co-organised the Sister March (Cardiff, 2017). Previously published in *Onward/Ymlaen!* and with the Red Poets, she performs annually at the Merthyr Rising Festival. Her work has appeared in Bloodaxe Books (2015), *The London Magazine* (2020) and *Tongue & Talk* (made in Manchester, for BBC Radio 4, 2021). Gemma has recently submitted her PhD: an emancipatory project exploring collective trauma, and transcendence. Entitled *Concrete Diamonds*, it's a hybrid novel, featuring an interwoven, eco-feminist mythopoeic tale punctuated with graffiti and punk-style concrete poetry. Essentially a polyphonic homage to working-class people living in post-industrial Britain, the work captures the life worlds of five generations and encompasses a range of literary styles: from steam-of-consciousness to polemic, melodic and poetic, gritty realist and dark comedic. Underpinned with critical theory, the novel illuminates the past origins and present conditions of poverty, discrimination, and subjugation of underrepresented and marginalised people.

Professor Kerry E. Howell holds the Chair of Governance in the Faculty of Business and Law at Northumbria University, UK. Through his research Professor Howell has generated scholarly expertise in areas relating to the philosophy of methodology, governance, leadership, EU policy and regulation as well as written texts with Nova Science Press, Palgrave McMillan Press, Beijing Scientific Press and Sage Publications. He has also edited a research text regarding corporate governance and ethics with Palgrave McMillan Press and is currently writing a monograph analysing leadership, culture, identity, and path-dependency in Wales. Professor Howell has also supervised over thirty research degrees to completion, produced numerous refereed journal articles and managed funded research projects for various public and private sector institutions.

Gareth Twamley is a Cardiff based poet with a background in performing arts. Before his progression into writing he appeared in numerous TV shows and had roles in two feature films. Since 2017 he has been an integral part of the local grassroots poetry scene. As well as performing his work at local venues, Gareth has performed at several UK festivals and has appeared at performance poetry competitions including The Frequency House Swansea Poetry Slam. He is known for his eclectic writing style and strong delivery, ranging from punk and political to uplifting and soulful. Gareth has also ghost-written lyrics for numerous local singers and hip-hop artists and continues to write bespoke poetry for weddings, funerals and other events. His favourite poets and influences locally are Ifor Thomas, Gemma June Howell, Will Ford, Zaru Johnson and Johnny Giles. From 2018 to 2020 Gareth devised and presented his own open mic event Lyrical Miracles and also curated and presented the very popular Word Asylum events which gained plaudits from local poets and audiences alike. Gareth is currently focussing on developing his writing style on the page and continues to produce work with publication now his main goal.

Fionn Wilson was born in South Shields, Tyne and Wear and spent her formative years in Newcastle upon Tyne in the Eighties. She remembers the time of Thatcher and the Miners' Strike vividly, witnessing the grinding poverty in the west end of the city where she grew up. She was raised, alongside her twin sister, by her mum who trained as a nurse at what was then the Newcastle General Hospital. She eventually gained a degree in English and Philosophy from the University of South Wales, living in Pontypridd and Cardiff and settling for a while near Swansea. She developed a real and lasting love for Wales, its people and culture. She started to paint in 2011 and is self-taught, and now lives in Enfield, London. Her work is figurative, with a bent towards portraiture. She has painted, amongst others, former MP Dennis Skinner, writer and left-wing historian Tariq Ali and the former General Secretary of the RMT, Bob Crow. Her urban landscapes focus on social alienation, despair and isolation. Her work forms part of public collections including the Marx Memorial Library, the National Coalmining Museum for England, the Museum of London and the Museum of Enfield.

J. Brookes was born in S.E. London in 1951. He has lived in Cardiff for thirty years, where, amongst other things, he edited the little poetry magazine, *The Yellow Crane*, for the ten years of its life. Parthian published his *New & Selected Poems: Hymns Ancient & Modern*, in 2019.

Dave Lewis is a Welsh, working-class writer, poet and photographer from the ex-mining village of Cilfynydd. He read Zoology at Cardiff University and has taught science, IT and photography. He has always lived in Wales apart from a year, teaching and volunteering in Kenya. He founded the International Welsh Poetry Competition, now the biggest poetry contest in Wales. He also runs the Writers of Wales database, the Poetry Book Awards, Wales Trails and book publishing company Publish & Print. All his projects are self-funded and he gets no support from anyone in the arts business. He has published over twenty books. His epic poem, *Roadkill*, deals with the class struggle and rants against injustice. His poetry collection, *Going Off Grid*, is concerned with the dangers of digital capitalism. His novel *The Welsh Man* touches the dark underbelly of 80s and 90s gangland Britain as seen through the eyes of a poor, working-class Welsh lad. His poetry has been published all over the world in various magazines and websites. Resolutely untrendy, he is shunned by the literature establishment in Wales but still works full-time as a writer. He also likes beer, photographing animals and travel.

Des Mannay is a member of a BAME family that originated in Cardiff's docks. A long-time community activist, and former shop steward in NALGO and the GMB, he has had articles published in *Socialist Worker, Socialist Review*, and was on the Editorial Board of the short-lived *Welsh Socialist Voice*, for which he also wrote. He is also a poet, and his first poetry collection, *Sod 'em—and tomorrow* is published by Waterloo Press. He is co-editor of *The Angry Manifesto* poetry journal and winner of the *rethinkyourmind* poetry competition (2015). He came second in the LIT-UP poetry competition (2019), and was highly commended for the Disability Arts Cymru Poetry Competition (2015). Des achieved the 'Gold Award' for the Creative Futures Literary Awards (2015) and was shortlisted in 7 competitions. He was a judge for the *Valiant Scribe* Vultures and Doves Poetry Competition (USA). Des has performed at numerous venues/festivals and has published in various poetry journals. His work appears in 36 poetry anthologies.

Taz Rahman is a Cardiff based professional wedding and portrait photographer as well as a poet. He is the founder of *Just Another Poet*, the first Youtube poetry channel in Wales. He was awarded a bursary and writing commission by Literature Wales in 2020 and has been editing the legal news blog LawNews Index.com since 2011.

Sierra Moulinié is a 35-year-old queer and nonbinary poet born and raised on a council estate in South Wales. They write primarily about their battles with mental health, as well as about LGBT issues and problems in modern society, and often performs at local open mic events.

Gustavius Payne was born in Merthyr Tydfil in 1969 and was raised during the 1970s and '80s on the nearby Gurnos estate. More interested in singing for a local punk band, he left school at sixteen, but returned to full-time education at 21 to pursue his interest in visual art. Payne won his first art prize soon after at the 1993 National Eisteddfod of Wales, as Student of the Year. He has worked on various community arts projects as artist, facilitator and/or development officer. As a fine artist he is interested in the human predicament. His figurative paintings use Nature, alongside hoodies, mobile phones, religious iconography, and other human constructs. Imagery from mythology and folklore, alongside ecological and political concerns, draws the viewer into a fascinating reflective world, set in the post-industrial Welsh Valleys. He is represented by Ffin-Y-Parc Gallery in Llanrwst, where his work is regularly shown and held in stock, as well as at various other galleries too. He has exhibited regularly since 1994, including an Arts Council of Wales-funded collaborative touring exhibition, Dim Gobaith Caneri (No Hope Canary), with poet and author Mike Jenkins, during 2011—2012.

Summar Jade is a 28-year-old performance artist. She was brought up in council housing and then from the age of sixteen she brought herself up, with the help of Gwalia Housing Association and Llety Llanelli foyer support staff, to whom she is eternally grateful. Her creative motivation is to express her trauma and emotions to inspire others to do the same.

Xavier Panadès i Blas was brought up in a peasant background and was educated to the revolutionary values of solidarity, justice, and freedom. This led Xavier to become involved in social-political and environmental movements since the mid 1980s. In fact, Xavier has been instrumental in the internationalisation of the culture of the Catalan Lands. he has been stunning audiences for the last 20 years with his explosive performances in Catalan around the globe, which is not surprising as Xavier's writings totally absorb the readers. His poems and stories are regularly published in international journals and in particular his poems in *The Ear of Eternity* (Francis Boutle: 2019) is an experience of self-discovery where the artist becomes insignificant, a mere channeller. Xavier is currently working on translating and setting to music poems by Ramon Folch i Camarasa, recording the poems for his upcoming album, and recording poets in Catalan, Castilian, and English for the non-profit organisation Listen to Poetry.

Jon Gower is a prize-winning author with over thirty books to his name. These include *The Story of Wales*, which accompanied the landmark BBC TV series and *Y Storïwr*, which won the Wales Book of the Year. His volume *An Island Called Smith*, about a disappearing island in Chesapeake Bay was awarded the John Morgan Travel Writing Prize. Recent publications include studies of the radical film-maker Karl Francis and the visual artist John Selway as well as *Gwalia Patagonia*, being an account of the Welsh settlement in Patagonia and *Wales: At Water's Edge* about the country's coastal path. Jon has also published five novels and five collections of short stories. He was an inaugural Hay Festival International Fellow and has been awarded an Arts Council of Wales Prize, a Creative Wales award and won both yhe National Eisteddfod Short Story Prize and the Allen Raine Short Story Competition.

Rob Mimpriss was inspired in his politics by Gwynfor Evans and Saunders Lewis, who reasserted the value of Welsh culture against the British state, and in his writing by Kate Roberts, Bernard Malamud and Raymond Carver, who used the short story to assert the dignity of ordinary lives. He is the author of four short-story collections, *Reasoning, For His Warriors, Prayer at the End*, and *Pugnacious Little Trolls*, and the editor of *Dangerous Asylums*, an anthology of fiction inspired by the history of Denbigh Hospital. He has translated from Welsh, among other things, the seventeenth-century classic, *A Book of Three Birds*, as a means to reflect on the interplay between Welsh and British loyalties and identities in the wake of Brexit. He lives near Bangor, Gwynedd.

Philip John is a Welsh poet, born and raised into a working-class family in the post-mining Rhondda Valleys. He descends from a family of coal miners and construction workers and was within the first generation to attend University. After graduating from the University of South Wales, he moved across the border to Bristol to work within procurement. Philip secured a publishing deal with Wordcatcher Publishing and his first poetry book, *Home Truths*, was published in November 2018. He has since released two further volumes: *Searching for Seahorses* (2020) and *Songs of Youth* (2021). His work reflects on his experiences of working-class Wales and he takes inspiration from its history. He explores the themes of social justice, the human condition, nature, and the environment. Philip has since returned to Wales and now resides in Monmouthshire. Through his writing, he is keen to express the struggle for equality and for a stronger political voice for his country and its people. To find out more, you can connect with Philip on his Facebook and Instagram pages by searching for @philipjohnpoetry.

Sarah Oneill is a single parent, ex horse trainer, and local artist from West Cross, Swansea. After a car accident, Sarah turned her attention to the canvas and took inspiration from her beloved horses, which she couldn't ride anymore. Years later, she successfully battled cancer, and uses the beautiful coastline as well as her faithful Welsh collie Bean as inspiration for her work, which helps her to express emotion and manage her mental health. Sarah works with acrylic and oils on canvas and has recently turned her hand to filming and directing short poetry films.

Jon Doyle's writing focuses on the impact of the late capitalist system on individuals and communities, and how it maintains its control and exploitation through various insidious means. His characters exist within a contemporary capitalist order, one able to subvert and subsume attempts to organise against it, destabilising the traditional narratives of solidarity and co-opting the symbols of protest. Confused and powerless, they are aware that things are not right or just but are unable to challenge them directly. Though fictionalised, *Be The Best* draws upon his experiences playing youth football for Cwmafan Boys Club in the mid-2000s. A version of the piece was first published by *Barren Magazine* in 2019. He was born and raised in Port Talbot, South Wales, where he lives today.

Margot Morgan. Swansea born in 1958 to Welsh and American parents, Margot Morgan was raised in New Jersey from the age of five. She returned to Swansea in 1976 where she studied for a BA, raised two children, and earned her living as a teacher while developing a parallel career in music. Margot has a passion for Wales as a Swansea 'Jackette', and as an outsider, and is a student of Welsh writing in English (MA). She has sung and performed with numerous drama and music groups and had several articles published with a focus on Wales. At Jazz Heritage Wales she promotes women in music, is a singer, and interpreted the poetry of Dylan Thomas for the Jen Wilson Ensemble which released the critically acclaimed *Twelve Poems: the Dylan Thomas Jazz Suite*. Margot has since gained an MA in Jazz Performance from RWCMD. She tutors English and singing, teaches, and is an Education Consultant and Deputy Chair for Jazz Heritage Wales at UWTSD.

H Raven Rose views art as alchemy capable of purging subliminal shadow before lifting the individual to sublime heights of consciousness. Her narrative approach is that of a shamanic storyteller and her visionary fiction includes symbols and elements meant to help readers and viewers transcend the mundane, positively transform their fractured psyche, or expand their consciousness. A writer-director, her poem painted in film, *Sacred Birthday, Sacred Wales—Pen-Blwydd yn Gysegredig, Cymru Sanctaidd*, won the 2021 Wales International Film Festival Illustrated Poem Jury's Award Special Prize. In 2018, her Super 8 short film *Sleep Disturbance* was shot in Bristol and screened at The Cube Microplex, UK. Her play *Dark Eros*, adapted into a suspense novelette of the same title, was staged as readings in Los Angeles, one of which starred Jessica Biel in the lead role as Leila. An excerpt of the play version of *Sleep Disturbance* was staged as readings at the Taliesin Create Space. Recent publications include creative nonfiction, *Waking up Wild* and *Snow*, published in Tofu Ink Arts Press, and an ecopoem, '23 Species from 19 States lost to extinction,' published in the Winter 2022 edition of *In Parentheses*.

Mike Jenkins is a retired teacher of English and Associate Editor at Culture Matters. He is an activist in Yes Cymru and previously Cymru Goch. Has co-edited *Red Poets* magazine for 28 years. Writer of novels, short stories and poetry. Latest books are *Anonymous Bosch* (Culture Matters) in Merthyr dialect with photos by Dave Lewis and April 2022, *Seams of People* (Carreg Gwalch). He is the editor of *Onward/ Ymlaen!* (Culture Matters), an anthology of radical poems from Cymru. Recently edited *Gwrthryfel/Uprising* (Culture Matters 2022), more radical poetry from Cymru.

Samantha Mansi is LGBTQIA, Swansea-based poet and left-wing activist, currently studying for an MA in Creative Writing. She works for POBL and is getting ready to launch a dogwalking and sitting business in the Swansea area. Samantha has been on a journey of healing from being culted, surviving trauma of abuse with inner-child healing, of which she has considerable expertise and knowledge. She took part in the Miss Mystic Pageant in 2021, achieving the Mystic Ambassador title, and featured in the adjoining charity calendar. Samamtha is currently writing a novel about her surviverhood and is hoping to publish It next year.

Karl Francis is from Bedwas in the Rhymney valley, and is an award-winning Welsh film and television director, producer, and screenwriter, associated with left-wing political causes. His output includes films in both English and Welsh, and uses both professional and amateur actors. In 2010 the BBC Wales art site selected his film *Above Us The Earth* as one of the ten greatest films about Wales, and in 2012, the BFI/UK Film Council selected *Above Us The Earth* as the best independent film ever made in Wales. In 1995 Karl was appointed the Head of Drama at BBC Wales, a role he held until 1997. Karl also won a British Academy Cymru Award for Director in 1991, for *Morphine & Dolly Mixtures* and in 1997, *Streetlife*, which featured Rhys Ifans and the late Helen McCrory, who received Best Actress for her performance.

Maj Ikle (Jane Campbell) is proud to be a dyke writer living off-grid in a handmade house in rural west Wales. Winner of the 2014 *Asian Cha* magazine competition with the poem 'The City Park,' Jane is an active member of the West Wales book festival and slam poetry circuit recently coming runner up in the Big Cwtch. Her short stories have been published in literary magazines such as *Storm Cellar* and *The Lampeter Review* as well as being in many anthologies and online.

Dr. Alys Einion is a true polymath. A writer, novelist, midwife and now Associate Professor of Midwifery at City, University of London, Fellow of the Royal College of Midwives, and Editor in Chief of the Practising Midwife Journal, she believes passionately in promoting equality and supporting women's and people's autonomy and rights, particularly in childbearing. She has published widely, including two novels with Honno, Welsh Women's Press and has contributed her academic work to several volumes relating to gender, sexuality, midwifery, motherhood, paganism, and women's relationships. As a public speaker she advocates for better understanding of the way stories shape our identities, and for improving the representation of women and birthing people. Alys is a passionate advocate for inclusive education and for LGBTQIA+ rights, and a staunchly inclusive feminist, and is the creator of Centred Birth Hypnobirthing. She is a vegan, pagan and proud mother to a grown-up son.

Philippa Brown was born in Cardiff and brought up down the docks. She's from a working-class family and has worked in bars and clubs most of her life. After the breakdown of her marriage, she decided to pursue her passion for art and completed an access course for the Cardiff Arts Academy, then moved to Swansea to complete her art degree. After living in Swansea for 8 years, she ran a Frieda Kahlo inspired art & vintage shop in Sketty, selling her work and vintage homeware. She now runs Viva La Frieda, in Morriston, a successful venture selling upcycled furniture and her work.

Zoe John is a doctoral researcher at Cardiff University's School of Social Sciences (SOCSI) and a criminology tutor at Swansea University. Her work explores the production and management of violence, embodiment, and gender in mixed martial arts (MMA) and uses a flexible researcher role to participate in MMA classes for research purposes. Zoe primarily draws from field notes as a point of discussion, noting the physically felt, the theoretically suggested, and observed experiences, as her position as 'woman', 'participant', and 'researcher'. Zoe has also worked with creative methodologies such as poetry as a form of data analysis and looks to publish this at a later point. Outside academia, she's passionate about discussing mental health and her experiences with suffering and recovering from eating disorders, and volunteers as an ambassador for BEAT where she discusses her story and has provided talks across the UK. Zoe is also interested in developing coaching knowledge/ experience in American football and Australian Rules Football (AFL).

John Frost has chosen to remain anonymous.

David Collyer is the winner of the RPS Documentary Photographer of the Year award (2021) for his images taken inside an NHS hospital during lockdown last year. David, who is an Operating Department Practitioner at Abergavenny's Nevill Hall hospital had discussed making a series of images about the workplace before Covid. The hospital was scheduled to lose its Emergency Department and acute surgical and medical care with the opening of a new hospital nearby. His images have appeared in national media outlets such as *The Guardian* to document the strain put on the NHS during the pandemic.

Rhys Trimble is a neurodiverse, bilingual poet, teacher, translator, performer, critic, musician, sound artist, visual artist, shaman, pastynwr, performance artist, publisher, editor and activist who provided a speech at the Banthebill protest in Bangor. Born in Zambia, raised in South Wales and resident in North Wales, he is the author of 20 or so books.

10 Within class ... to the challenge